**TEACHER'S PET PUBLICATIONS**

LITPLAN TEACHER PACK
for
A Tale of Two Cities
based on the book by
Charles Dickens

Written by
Mary B. Collins

© 1996 Teacher's Pet Publications
All Rights Reserved

This **LitPlan** for Charles Dickens'
Tale of Two Cities
has been brought to you by Teacher's Pet Publications, Inc.

Copyright Teacher's Pet Publications 1996
11504 Hammock Point
Berlin MD 21811

Only the student materials in this unit plan (such as worksheets,
study questions, and tests) may be reproduced multiple times
for use in the purchaser's classroom.

For any additional copyright questions,
contact Teacher's Pet Publications.

www.tpet.com

TABLE OF CONTENTS - *A Tale of Two Cities*

Introduction	9
Unit Objectives	12
Reading Assignment Sheet	13
Unit Outline	14
Study Questions (Short Answer)	17
Quiz/Study Questions (Multiple Choice)	27
Pre-reading Vocabulary Worksheets	45
Lesson One (Introductory Lesson)	63
Oral Reading Evaluation Form	66
Writing Assignment 1	71
Writing Assignment 2	74
Writing Assignment 3	85
Writing Evaluation Form	86
Vocabulary Review Activities	79
Extra Writing Assignments/Discussion ?s	82
Unit Review Activities	87
Unit Tests	91
Unit Resource Materials	129
Vocabulary Resource Materials	145

A FEW NOTES ABOUT THE AUTHOR
CHARLES DICKENS

DICKENS, Charles (1812-70). On a pier in New York Harbor in 1841 a crowd watched a tall sailing ship from England being towed to the pierhead. There was no ocean communication cable as yet and the ship brought the latest news. A question was yelled from the pier to the ship: "Is Little Nell dead?" Little Nell was the heroine in a serial called 'Old Curiosity Shop'. The latest installment was on the ship, and the people were anxious to learn how the story came out.

The author who could stir people to such excitement was Charles Dickens, then a young man of 29. The next year, on his visit to America, he received a reception second only to that of Lafayette in 1824. Six years before, with his 'Pickwick Papers', he had become the world's most celebrated writer.

Charles Dickens was born on Feb. 7, 1812, in Portsmouth. His father, John Dickens, was a minor clerk in the navy offices, a friendly man with a large family (Charles was the second of eight children) and only a moderate income. The family drifted from one poor home in London to another, each shabbier than the last. Presently John Dickens ended up in the Marshalsea Prison for debt and took his wife and younger children with him.

Meanwhile young Charles worked in a ramshackle warehouse, lived in a garret, visited his family in prison on Sundays, and felt that his life was shattered before it had begun. For a fictionalized account of his early life, read 'David Copperfield'. Then a timely inheritance restored the family to something like comfortable means, and Charles had a few quiet years at a private school.

Later he immortalized his father, for whom he always had a great love, as Mr. Micawber. When his own rising fortune and fame gave him control of a great newspaper, he put his father on the staff to preside over the dispatches and bought him a small country house. Dickens' mother, unsympathetic and unconscious of his genius, meant less to him; she begrudged his leaving work to go to school. He made her immortal as Mrs. Nickleby.

Dickens made his own career. A few years of secondary school was his basic education. He never attended college. His real education came from his reading and observation and daily experience. Except for the English novels of the 18th century, he knew little of great literature. Of history and foreign politics, he knew practically nothing. His novels all deal with his own day and his own environment, except for his two historical novels-'A Tale of Two Cities' and 'Barnaby Rudge'-and these were set in the recent past of the French Revolution and the Gordon Riots.

The qualities that made up Dickens' genius did not depend on formal education for development. Dickens had a reporter's eye for the details of daily life and a mimic's ear for the subtleties of common speech. Further, he had the artist's ability to select what he needed from these raw materials of observation and to shape them into works of enduring merit.

Preparation for a Career

By teaching himself shorthand, Dickens secured the position of court reporter in the old Doctors' Commons, a survival from Elizabethan days that handled marriage, divorce, wills, and other "ghostly" causes. This experience gave Dickens a peculiar dislike of law that never left him; forever after it seemed either comic as in "Bardell vs. Pickwick" or terrible with tragedy as in 'Bleak House'. Dickens moved up in 1831 to the Reporters' Gallery of the "old-the unburned and unreformed-House of Commons." He also went to other cities and towns to report election speeches, transcribing his notes on the palm of his hand "by the light of a dark lantern in a post-chaise and four." This experience gave him a detailed and sometimes cynical view of government. To him the voters were often represented by the Eatanswill Election in 'Pickwick', parliamentary government by Doodle and Foodle and Coodle ('Our Mutual Friend'), and civil service by the Circumlocution Office ('Little Dorrit').

Thus equipped, Charles Dickens set out to conquer the world. The stage was his first dream. Night after night for two or three years he sat entranced with the melodrama of the London theaters-lurid with love, battle, treachery, and blue fire, in which a heroic young man would knock over 16 smugglers like ninepins. Melodrama put a stamp on Dickens for life. His characters, if they get excited, drop into the ranting language of the old Adelphi Theatre. On the other hand, Dickens' intense concentration on acting helped to give him that weird, almost hypnotic, power that he showed in the public reading of his works.

However, fate led him to a different career. He had a passion for creative writing, and he has told of his great joy, of his eyes dimmed with tears when a manuscript sent anonymously to an editor appeared in print. So he began writing sketches under the name of "Boz," the family nickname of a younger brother. To "Boz" came sudden and great success. The publishers, Chapman and Hall, had a plan for some serial pictures of cockney sportsmen, a Nimrod club, having all sorts of misadventures. The humor of the period turned very much on such horseplay. An artist named Seymour had drawn one or two pictures. They asked young "Boz" to write a set of stories to go with the pictures. Knowing nothing of sport, Dickens suggested changing the activities of the Nimrod club from sport to travel. When the publishers agreed, then, says Dickens, "I thought of Mr. Pickwick," which is all that has ever been known of the origin and genesis of one of the greatest characters in humorous literature. The young author was to receive 14 guineas (about $70) for each monthly installment.

The very week that the 'Pickwick Papers' began their monthly appearance, in April 1836, Dickens married Catherine Hogarth, one of the three pretty daughters of a newspaper associate. The young couple moved into rooms in Furnival's Inn. They did not realize that one day they would separate with bitter words because they believed they had made a love match. Dickens looked on Catherine, beautiful and silent, and saw nothing but the reflection of himself.

Catherine looked at Charles and did not realize that genius and egotism often lie close together. Dickens indeed was not so much in love with Catherine as in love with love.

At first the 'Pickwick Papers' failed to sell more than a few hundred copies a month. Then the serial introduced the character of Mr. Sam Weller, polishing boots at the White Hart Inn. The narrative took off on the wings of imagination, down English lanes, past gabled inns, and along the highways as varied and as cheery as a flying coach at a gallop, and the world was at the author's feet. The phenomenal 'Pickwick Papers' and the books that followed steadily lifted young "Boz" to the height of success, from poverty to wealth, from obscurity to fame, all in a few brief years. The great novels of this period were 'Oliver Twist' (published in 1838), 'Nicholas Nickleby' (1839), 'Old Curiosity Shop' (1841), and 'Barnaby Rudge' (1841).

Dickens in America

Dickens now looked around for other worlds to conquer. America had welcomed his books from the start, in part because the lack of international copyright permitted American publishers to print them without paying him. Dickens, in his youth a radical who hated Toryism and aristocracy, longed to study America and its freedom at first hand. Leaving their four children at home, he landed with his wife in Boston in January 1842. The town blazed with excitement; society was thrilled; there were dinners, receptions, adulation. Young Dickens, dressed in a bright velvet waistcoat, reveled in his new and adoring audience and wrote home of the freedom of America and the comforts of the workers. H.W. Longfellow, William Ellery Channing, and others of the New England elite joined in the welcome. Young Dr. Oliver Wendell Holmes was one of those who helped to organize it.

Dickens found in Boston friendships that he never lost, even when bitterness and disillusion altered his view of America. From Boston he went to New York and a "Boz" ball of 3,000 people; to Philadelphia and a huge public reception; then to Baltimore and to Washington, where he met President John Tyler and the Congress; then to Richmond, which offered him a taste of Southern culture. Such was the triumphant progress of the young author, only a few years before a member of the shabby-genteel class of London.

Always ready to raise his voice in defense of a cause he believed in, Dickens spoke everywhere of the need for an international copyright agreement that would protect the rights of both American and British writers. He felt that it was unfair and unjust that American publishers should print and sell his books without permission from him and without paying him any royalties. Dickens did not speak of himself as the sole victim of this practice. He pointed out that all British authors were equally victimized; he also acknowledged that American authors, such as Edgar Allan Poe, suffered from the pirating of their works in England.

The newspapers in America attacked these forthright statements and accused Dickens of bad taste and of abusing American hospitality. In time Dickens' rosy view of America faded. The proof of his disillusion and disgust is revealed in his 'American Notes' (published in 1842), his letters to friends, and 'Martin Chuzzlewit' (1844). From Dickens' viewpoint, Americans all seemed to chew tobacco. They kept slaves, whom he never stopped to compare with the factory slaves of England. American government seemed all plunder and roguery. Then he went West, traveling as far as Cairo, Ill. His vision of the West contained nothing but foul and reeking canal boats, swamps, bullfrogs, and tobacco juice.

Dickens lacked the eye to see the pageant of America, the great epic of the settlements of the West; the eye to compare the canal boat with the raft and the scow of earlier settlers. He became peevish, impatient of small discomforts, resenting the fact that hotelkeepers dared to talk to him. He spent two weeks in Canada, consoled there by the presence of friends at the English garrison in Montreal. Then he returned home to discredit America with his pen.

Fame and Fortune

The years that followed Dickens' return from America-the middle period of his life-were filled with more activity, fame, and success. In 1851 he took a fine residence at Tavistock Square and lived in great style. His friends were the leading authors, artists, and actors of the day. Later on, his purchase of a country house at Gad's Hill fulfilled an ambition of his childhood. His books, appearing in monthly serial parts, enjoyed a popularity that slackened only to rise again. It is generally thought that 'David Copperfield', written as a serial in 1848 and 1849, when he was at the height of his powers, is the greatest of his novels. Contrasted with the 'Pickwick Papers', it shows the transition of Dickens' genius from the exuberance of youth to the somber acceptance of middle age.

One of his books, 'Dombey and Son', is a sort of epic of great sorrow. Dickens' books indeed appealed to his generation of readers as much for their tears as for their laughter.

Reformer-Journalist

Book writing did not entirely satisfy Dickens' ego. The onetime reporter wanted to be a newspaper editor. Dickens felt the need to reform all England. The way to do it, he felt, was to control and edit a great daily newspaper, where he should preside like Jupiter handing out lightning. Enthusiastic friends subscribed £100,000 and founded the Daily News. In January 1846 Dickens threw himself eagerly into the editorial chair of the fledgling publication and threw himself out again in 19 days. He found that in the newspaper business the lightning hits in two directions. So in 1850 he founded instead a weekly journal, Household Words, and carried on with it and a later magazine, All the Year Round (1859), until his death. Several of his own stories, 'Christmas Stories', 'A Tale of Two Cities', 'Great Expectations', and others ran in his magazine.

Dickens as Actor and Lecturer

Another activity, and this a special delight to him, was amateur theatricals that carried on Dickens' love of the stage. He himself had incomparable dramatic power. With it he had a great talent for management and an energy and enthusiasm that carried all before it. On May 16, 1851, at a performance that was given at the duke of Devonshire's London house for a charity, the young Queen Victoria and her Prince Consort and the duke of Wellington were in the audience.

The queen came to a later performance in 1857 and graciously "commanded Mr. Dickens' presence"-an invitation of great honor-after the show. Mr. Dickens being in "farce" dress asked to be excused from appearing, thus defying all royal precedents.

To theatricals he soon added public lectures and readings from his works. This activity began after he had read one of his famous Christmas stories to a group of friends who received it enthusiastically. He made a number of successful tours in England, Scotland, and Ireland-from 1858 to 1859, 1861 to 1863, 1866 to 1867, and 1869 to 1870.

Relief in Work

Dickens separated from his wife in 1858. Georgina Hogarth, his wife's younger sister, had lived with the couple since 1842. She remained with Dickens until his death. His will provided for both women.

Dickens sought relief from a public curious about his personal life in the excitement of work. He made a second American tour in 1867 to 1868. It was an overwhelming success but extremely fatiguing. At home again, he resumed lecturing. His last appearance was in March 1870.

In retirement he struggled with his last task, 'The Mystery of Edwin Drood', a tale of night and storm and murder. The book was still unfinished on June 9, 1870, when Dickens died.

In the opinion of many, Dickens is England's greatest creative writer. The names and natures of his characters are unforgettable. His humor is unsurpassable, not only in the laughter that lies on the surface, but in the warmth of human kindliness below. His books are still being read all over the world. 'A Christmas Carol', conceived and written in a few weeks in 1843, is the ultimate, enduring Christmas myth of modern literature.

--- Courtesy of Compton's Learning Company

INTRODUCTION

This unit has been designed to develop students' reading, writing, thinking, and language skills through exercises and activities related to *A Tale of Two Cities* by Charles Dickens. It includes eighteen lessons, supported by extra resource materials.

The **introductory lesson** introduces students to the fact that in the next several weeks they will be working with, among other things, the two cities of Paris and London. Following the introductory activity, students are given a transition to explain how the activity relates to the book they are about to read. Following the transition, students are given the materials they will be using during the unit. At the end of the lesson, students begin the pre-reading work for the first reading assignment.

The **reading assignments** are approximately thirty pages each; some are a little shorter while others are a little longer. Students have approximately 15 minutes of pre-reading work to do prior to each reading assignment. This pre-reading work involves reviewing the study questions for the assignment and doing some vocabulary work for 8 to 10 vocabulary words they will encounter in their reading.

The **study guide questions** are fact-based questions; students can find the answers to these questions right in the text. These questions come in two formats: short answer or multiple choice. The best use of these materials is probably to use the short answer version of the questions as study guides for students (since answers will be more complete), and to use the multiple choice version for occasional quizzes. If your school has the appropriate equipment, it might be a good idea to make transparencies of your answer keys for the overhead projector.

The **vocabulary work** is intended to enrich students' vocabularies as well as to aid in the students' understanding of the book. Prior to each reading assignment, students will complete a two-part worksheet for approximately 8 to 10 vocabulary words in the upcoming reading assignment. Part I focuses on students' use of general knowledge and contextual clues by giving the sentence in which the word appears in the text. Students are then to write down what they think the words mean based on the words' usage. Part II nails down the definitions of the words by giving students dictionary definitions of the words and having students match the words to the correct definitions based on the words' contextual usage. Students should then have a thorough understanding of the words when they meet them in the text.

After each reading assignment, students will go back and formulate answers for the study guide questions. Discussion of these questions serves as a **review** of the most important events and ideas presented in the reading assignments.

After students complete reading the work, there is a **vocabulary review** lesson which pulls together all of the fragmented vocabulary lists for the reading assignments and gives students a review of all of the words they have studied.

The **group activity** which follows the vocabulary review has students working in small groups to discuss the main themes of the novel. Using the information they have acquired so far through individual work and class discussions, students get together to further examine the text and to brainstorm ideas relating to the themes of the novel.

After completing their group work, students have a **reporting and discussion** session in which the groups share their ideas about the themes with the entire class; thus, the entire class is exposed to information about all of the themes and the entire class can discuss each theme based on the nucleus of information brought forth by each of the groups.

Following the group activity, a lesson is devoted to the **extra discussion questions/writing assignments**. These questions focus on interpretation, critical analysis and personal response, employing a variety of thinking skills and adding to the students' understanding of the novel.

There are three **writing assignments** in this unit, each with the purpose of informing, persuading, or having students express personal opinions. The first assignment is to inform: each student writes a report detailing exactly what he/she did for and contributed to the group project. The second assignment is to express personal opinions: students have a choice of various assignments, using either fact or fiction, to express their own opinions about their own towns or cities. The third assignment is to persuade: students compare and contrast their own cities/towns with either Paris or London and either persuade a person who lives in Paris or London to come to their city to live -- or -- persuade a friend to move with them to Paris or London.

The **nonfiction reading assignment** for this unit is integrated into the group project assignment. Students are divided into two groups: half of the class are Parisians, the other half are Londoners. Each group researches and prepares a multi-media presentation about its city.

The **review lesson** pulls together all of the aspects of the unit. The teacher is given four or five choices of activities or games to use which all serve the same basic function of reviewing all of the information presented in the unit.

The **unit test** comes in two formats: multiple choice or short answer. As a convenience, two different tests for each format have been included. There is an advanced short answer unit test.

There are additional **support materials** included with this unit. The **extra activities packet** includes suggestions for an in-class library, crossword and word search puzzles related to the novel, and extra vocabulary worksheets. There is a list of **bulletin board ideas** which gives the teacher suggestions for bulletin boards to go along with this unit. In addition, there is a list of **extra class activities** the teacher could choose from to enhance the unit or as a substitution for an exercise the teacher might feel is inappropriate for his/her class. **Answer keys** are located directly after the **reproducible student materials** throughout the unit. The student materials may be reproduced for use in the teacher's classroom without infringement of copyrights. No other portion of this unit may be reproduced without the written consent of Teacher's Pet Publications, Inc.

UNIT OBJECTIVES - *A Tale of Two Cities*

1. Through reading Charles Dickens's *A Tale of Two Cities*, students will learn about Paris and London, and they will also take a fresh look at their own cities or towns.

2. Students will demonstrate their understanding of the text on four levels: factual, interpretive, critical and personal.

3. Students will be exposed to a bit of world history and learn about the French Revolution.

4. Students will examine the themes of revenge, rich versus poor, coincidence, and being "recalled to life."

5. Students will use logic to put together pieces of the plot to resolve the relationships and motives in the novel.

6. Students will be given the opportunity to practice reading aloud and silently to improve their skills in each area.

7. Students will answer questions to demonstrate their knowledge and understanding of the main events and characters in *A Tale of Two Cities* as they relate to the author's theme development.

8. Students will enrich their vocabularies and improve their understanding of the novel through the vocabulary lessons prepared for use in conjunction with the novel.

9. The writing assignments in this unit are geared to several purposes:
    a. To have students demonstrate their abilities to inform, to persuade, or to express their own personal ideas
    Note: Students will demonstrate ability to write effectively to <u>inform</u> by developing and organizing facts to convey information. Students will demonstrate the ability to write effectively to <u>persuade</u> by selecting and organizing relevant information, establishing an argumentative purpose, and by designing an appropriate strategy for an identified audience. Students will demonstrate the ability to write effectively to <u>express personal ideas</u> by selecting a form and its appropriate elements.
    b. To check the students' reading comprehension
    c. To make students think about the ideas presented by the novel
    d. To encourage logical thinking
    e. To provide an opportunity to practice good grammar and improve students' use of the English language.

READING ASSIGNMENT SHEET - *A Tale of Two Cities*

Date to be Assigned	Chapters	Completion Date
	I(1-4)	
	I(5-6)	
	II(1-4)	
	II(5-8)	
	II(9-12)	
	II(13-16)	
	II(17-21)	
	II(22-24)	
	III(1-4)	
	III(5-8)	
	III(9-11)	
	III(12-15)	

UNIT OUTLINE - *A Tale of Two Cities*

1	2	3	4	5
Introduction PV I(1-4)	Read I(1-4) PV I(5-6)	Study ?s I(1-4) Read I(5-6) PV II(1-4)	Study ?s I(5-6) Project Work Read II(1-4)	Study ?s II(1-4) Library PVR II(5-8)
6	7	8	9	10
Study?sII(5-8) PV&R II(9-12)	Study ?sII(9-12) Group Work PVR II(13-16)	Study ?s II(13-16) Writing Assignment #2 PVR II(17-21)	Study ?s II(17-21) PVR II(22-24)	Study?s II(22-24) First Group Presentation PVR III(1-4)
11	12	13	14	15
Study ?s III(1-4) Second Group Presentation PVR III (5-8)	Study ?s III(5-8) Third Group Presentation PVR III(9-11)	Study ?s III (9-11) Fourth Group Presentation PVR III (12-15)	Study ?s III(12-15) Fifth Group Presentation	Sixth Group Presentation
16	17	18	19	20
Vocabulary	Group Activity	Reports & Discussion	Writing Assignment #3	Review Writing Conferences
21				
Test				

Key: P = Preview Study Questions   V = Prereading Vocabulary Worksheets   R = Read

SHORT ANSWER STUDY GUIDE QUESTIONS - *A Tale of Two Cities*

I(1-4)
1. Dickens describes England and France in 1775. How does he compare them? (1)
2. Both kings are described as having large jaws; what is Dickens telling us about them? (1)
3. Why are the Dover mail drivers and passengers so apprehensive of each other? (2)
4. How does Dickens describe human beings? (3)
5. Explain the meaning of "recalled to life." (4)
6. Identify Jarvis Lorry. (4)
7. Why does Lucie faint upon hearing Mr. Lorry's story? (4)

I (5-6)
1. Dickens uses the broken cask of wine's spilling in the street to foreshadow what future event? (5)
2. What is the significance of so many "Jacques" in Defarge's wine shop? (5)
3. Who are seen peeping through a hole in the wall at Dr. Manette? (5)
4. Why has Defarge allowed them to look in? (5)
5. What is Dr. Manette doing when Mr. Lorry and Lucie first see him? (5)
6. Describe Madame Defarge. (6)
7. What is Dr. Manette's mental state? (6)
8. Identify One Hundred and Five, North Tower. (6)
9. How does Lucie react to Dr. Manette? (6)

II (1-4)
1. What does Jerry Cruncher object to his wife doing? (1)
2. Who is Charles Darnay? (2)
3. Identify Mr. Stryver. (3)
4. Who is Mr. Carton? (3)
5. Why is Darnay acquitted? (3)
6. How does Mr. Carton feel about himself? (4)

II (5-8)
1. What name does Stryver call Carton? (5)
2. What words does Dickens use to describe Stryver and Carton? (5)
3. What does Carton actually do for Stryver? (5)
4. How does Dickens describe the Manettes' home? (6)
5. How does Dickens describe the privileged class in France? (7)
6. What feelings does Monsieur the Marquis have toward the child his carriage has run down? (7)
7. What is the countryside of France like? (8)

A Tale of Two Cities Short Answer Study Guide Page 2

II (9-12)
1. Charles visits his uncle the Marquis and informs him that he renounces his name and property. Why does Charles Darnay do this? (9)
2. In the conversation between the Marquis and Charles, Dickens gives a hint that at one time the Marquis was able to have someone imprisoned. Who? (9)
3. Why was the Marquis killed? (9)
4. Why doesn't Dr. Manette want Charles to reveal his true name? (10)
5. How does Stryver view his marriage to Lucie? (11)
6. Describe Carton's responses to Stryver's self-flattery. (11)
7. How does Stryver react to the certainty that his suit will fail? (12)

II (13-16)
1. What promise does Sydney Carton make to Lucie? (13)
2. What "fish" does Cruncher go fishing after? (14)
3. Why are Cruncher's fingers always rusty? (14)
4. Who was the doomed man the road-mender told the Jacques about? (15)
5. What register does Madame Defarge keep? (15)
6. Why does Madame Defarge wear a rose in her hair? (16)
7. Why is it ironic that John Barsad should come that particular day? (16)
8. Who else's name is Madame Defarge knitting? (16)

II (17-21)
1. Why does Dr. Manette cobble for nine days after Lucie and Charles are married? (18)
2. What does Dr. Manette allow Lorry and Miss Pross to do? (19)
3. Why does Lucie ask her husband to speak kindly toward Carton? (20)
4. Lucie's fanciful thought years ago of the echoes of a multitude of footsteps becomes a reality in France. What has occurred? (21)
5. What metaphor does Dickens use to describe the mob?
6. Who is The Vengeance? (21)

II (22-24)
1. Why was grass put in Foulon's mouth? (22)
2. Why does Mr. Lorry have to go to Paris? (24)
3. Why does Darnay go to France? (24)
4. Why is it foolish of Charles Darnay to go to France? (24)

A Tale of Two Cities Short Answer Study Guide Page 3

III (1-4)
1. Why is Charles imprisoned? (1)
2. Why does the crowd at the grindstone take up Dr. Manette's cause to free Charles? (2)
3. Why does Madame Defarge wish to see Lucie and the younger Lucie? (3)
4. What change has occurred within Dr. Manette? (4)

III (5-8)
1. What is the Carmagnole? (5)
2. What caused the jury to acquit Charles? (6)
3. How must Miss Pross and Jerry Cruncher perform the household shopping? Why? (7)
4. Why is Charles arrested again on the day of his release? (7)
5. Where does Miss Pross find her brother? (8)
6. Who identifies Solomon Pross as John Barsad? (8)
7. What does Carton want from Solomon Pross (Barsad)? (8)

III (9-11)
1. Why is Mr. Lorry appalled at Cruncher?
2. What arrangement has Carton made with Barsad? (9)
3. Dr. Manette worked to free Darnay during the first imprisonment. Who appears to be quietly working now? (9)
4. Who is the other person that the court claims has denounced Darnay? (9)
5. Who is Madame Defarge in Dr. Manette's letter? (10)
6. Why is Charles condemned to die? (10)
7. How has Carton changed since he landed in France? (11)

III (12-15)
1. Where does Madame Defarge plan to end her vengeance? (12)
2. Why does Carton have Darnay write the letter? (13)
3. How does Cruncher change? (14)
4. Why is Miss Pross in a "queer condition"? (14)
5. Sydney Carton said he would die young because of a dissipated and wasted life. How was he both right and wrong? (15)
6. How is Madame Defarge cheated? (15)
7. What words about the future are attributed to Carton at the end of the novel? (15)

ANSWER KEY SHORT ANSWER STUDY GUIDE QUESTIONS - *A Tale of Two Cities*

I(1-4)

1. Dickens describes England and France in 1775. How does he compare them? (1)
    Both are ruled by kings who enjoy divine right and appear to believe the status quo is not only unimpeachable but everlasting as well.

2. Both kings are described as having large jaws; what is Dickens telling us about them? (1)
    They appear to be interchangeable and full of empty talk. He implies that they are stupid men who are out of touch with the real world inhabited by their subjects.

3. Why are the Dover mail drivers and passengers so apprehensive of each other? (2)
    They all fear robbery and murder by highwaymen and that one of them may even be an accomplice.

4. How does Dickens describe human beings? (3)
    We are a secret and a mystery to each other, even those we love.

5. Explain the meaning of "recalled to life." (4)
    A man has been released after 18 years in prison in France.

6. Identify Jarvis Lorry. (4)
    Mr. Lorry is an elderly gentleman from Tellson's Bank in London. He brought Lucie Manette to England after her mother's death, but he has not seen her since.

7. Why does Lucie faint upon hearing Mr. Lorry's story? (4)
    She learns her father is alive and has been in prison for eighteen years while she thought he was dead. She and Mr. Lorry are to bring him to England. This information is quite a shock to her.

I (5-6)

1. Dickens uses the broken cask of wine's spilling in the street to foreshadow what future event? (5)
    The time will come when blood will be spilled in the streets and people will be stained with it as they are stained with the spilled wine.

2. What is the significance of so many "Jacques" in Defarge's wine shop? (5)
    They are using the name "Jacque" as a common name for members of the revolution.

3. Who are seen peeping through a hole in the wall at Dr. Manette? (5)
    The three Jacques from the wine shop are seen looking in at Dr. Manette.

4. Why has Defarge allowed them to look in? (5)
    He says that the sight is likely to do them good; anger will feed the coming revolution.

5. What is Dr. Manette doing when Mr. Lorry and Lucie first see him? (5)
   He is making shoes in a dark little room near the wine shop.

6. Describe Madame Defarge. (6)
   She is tall, wears furs and jewelry, and is constantly knitting. She appears to be aware of all that is occurring around her, even though she doesn't often actually appear to be watching.

7. What is Dr. Manette's mental state? (6)
   His mind has focused on only one task to the exclusion of everything else.

8. Identify One Hundred and Five, North Tower. (6)
   That is Dr. Manette's old cell number which has come to be his identity.

9. How does Lucie react to Dr. Manette? (6)
   She is at first frightened but is quickly overcome with compassion and love. She is able to bring back some old memories of her mother for Dr. Manette, but he is very confused. She holds him in her arms to make him well.

II (1-4)

1. What does Jerry Cruncher object to his wife doing? (1)
   He doesn't want her to pray, which he calls "flopping."

2. Who is Charles Darnay? (2)
   He is a young man being tried for treason. He apparently met with Lucie, Mr. Lorry and Dr. Manette on their way back to England, for they are called to testify in the case.

3. Identify Mr. Stryver. (3)
   He is Charles Darnay's attorney.

4. Who is Mr. Carton? (3)
   Carton is Stryver's associate.

5. Why is Darnay acquitted? (3)
   He and Mr. Carton resemble each other so that the prosecutor's witness was confused and therefore could not positively identify Darnay.

6. How does Mr. Carton feel about himself? (4)
   He is a disappointment to himself and feels unworthy of love.

II (5-8)

1. What name does Stryver call Carton? (5)
   He calls him Memory.

2. What words does Dickens use to describe Stryver and Carton? (5)
    He calls them Lion and Jackal.

3. What does Carton actually do for Stryver? (5)
    He does the thinking and research for him; he prepares Stryver's cases.

4. How does Dickens describe the Manettes' home? (6)
    It is sunny and cheery; almost like an oasis in an otherwise oppressed country.

5. How does Dickens describe the privileged class in France? (7)
    They are extravagant, superficial, and completely useless. They feel a false safety in their cocoon of perfect dress and manners. Dickens uses religious terms to illustrate their idea that the way they live is somehow sanctified from above.

6. What feelings does Monsieur the Marquis have toward the child his carriage has run down? (7)
    None. He regards the common people as less than animals. He is only disconcerted when one of the gold coins he threw down for compensation is thrown back into his carriage.

7. What is the countryside of France like? (8)
    The fields have the same starved and withered look as the people have.

II (9-12)

1. Charles visits his uncle the Marquis and informs him that he renounces his name and property. Why does Charles Darnay do this? (9)
    His mother's dying wish was that Charles would redress the family's many wrongs and cruelties, and that he would lighten the burden of his subjects in the village.

2. In the conversation between the Marquis and Charles, Dickens gives a hint that at one time the Marquis was able to have someone imprisoned. Who? (9)
    Dr. Manette was the "someone." The Marquis mentions the doctor and his daughter to Charles.

3. Why was the Marquis killed? (9)
    The common people rose up against him for running down the child and his careless attitude about the incident.

4. Why doesn't Dr. Manette want Charles to reveal his true name? (10)
    He suspects a connection between his past imprisonment and Charles' family; remember that Charles has felt the doctor looks at him with hate and fear at times. Perhaps the doctor sees a family resemblance.

5. How does Stryver view his marriage to Lucie? (11)
    He sees it as the possession of a pretty object who will be pleased to marry such a distinguished and gallant gentleman.

6. Describe Carton's responses to Stryver's self-flattery. (11)
   Carton stabs him with ironic jabs which completely pass over Stryver's head. Carton sees Stryver as he is: a bore who is puffed-up with his own self-importance.

7. How does Stryver react to the certainty that his suit will fail? (12)
   He congratulates himself that he is rid of a silly, flighty female who will probably come to an impoverished end. He thinks she is foolish not to be awed by his stature and importance and that this proves she is unworthy of him.

II (13-16)
1. What promise does Sydney Carton make to Lucie? (13)
   He promises that he would sacrifice himself for those she loves.

2. What "fish" does Cruncher go fishing after? (14)
   He "fishes" for the bodies of recently deceased people to sell to "scientific" buyers.

3. Why are Cruncher's fingers always rusty? (14)
   They are rusty from using his shovel and crowbar on his fishing expeditions.

4. Who was the doomed man the road-mender told the Jacques about? (15)
   The road-mender meant the man who stabbed the Marquis.

5. What register does Madame Defarge keep? (15)
   She knits the names of those who are enemies to the common people who have been tortured and killed. Her register is a long, knitted shroud.

6. Why does Madame Defarge wear a rose in her hair? (16)
   The rose is a signal that a spy is in the shop.

7. Why is it ironic that John Barsad should come that particular day? (16)
   It is the day Madame Defarge is knitting his name into the register.

8. Who else's name is Madame Defarge knitting? (16)
   She is knitting Charles Darnay's name.

II (17-21)
1. Why does Dr. Manette cobble for nine days after Lucie and Charles are married? (18)
   He learned that Charles was related to the Marquis, the man who imprisoned him. (At the end of the novel, we also can assume that at this point, Manette knows how deeply his daughter will be hurt if the letter he left in the prison is ever found.) His way of escaping this complication is to cobble.

2. What does Dr. Manette allow Lorry and Miss Pross to do? (19)
   He allows them to destroy his workbench.

3. Why does Lucie ask her husband to speak kindly toward Carton? (20)
　　She has seen that he has a good heart and is full of suffering.

4. Lucie's fanciful thought years ago of the echoes of a multitude of footsteps becomes a reality in France. What has occurred? (21)
　　The storming of the Bastille by the mob in Paris has taken place.

5. What metaphor does Dickens use to describe the mob?
　　He calls it a surging sea representing it in terms of ceaseless and unstoppable destruction.

6. Who is The Vengeance? (21)
　　She is Madame Defarge's lieutenant, a woman just as determined to bring down the nobility as M. Defarge.

II (22-24)

1. Why was grass put in Foulon's mouth? (22)
　　He had told the starving people to go eat grass.

2. Why does Mr. Lorry have to go to Paris? (24)
　　Because of the revolution, Tellson's Bank needs a man with experience to help order the business of the French branch. Mr. Lorry had worked in the French house for years when he was younger, so he is the logical one to go.

3. Why does Darnay go to France? (24)
　　Gabelle has been imprisoned for his association with Darnay's family, and Charles thinks he can help him.

4. Why is it foolish of Charles Darnay to go to France? (24)
　　He is a member of the nobility, and even though he has renounced his title, he puts himself in grave danger by returning to France at this time.

III (1-4)

1. Why is Charles imprisoned? (1)
　　He is imprisoned for being an emigrant and an aristocrat.

2. Why does the crowd at the grindstone take up Dr. Manette's cause to free Charles? (2)
　　Because he was once a prisoner at the Bastille, Dr. Manette is a sort of a folk hero. Anyone imprisoned by the old regime is automatically supported and admired.

3. Why does Madame Defarge wish to see Lucie and the younger Lucie? (3)
　　She wants to remember what they look like so that she can register them just as she registered all those names in her knitting.

4. What change has occurred within Dr. Manette? (4)

> He has become strong again. Having been a Bastille prisoner earns him the respect of the people, also his good tending of the sick during the period sets him apart. He walks through the revolution's atrocities somehow untouched, never suspected, always admired. He feels that his long years of confinement ". . . all tended to a good end" in that he had the power and influence to help Charles. In a sense his life has come full circle and returned his manhood to him.

III (5-8)

1. What is the Carmagnole? (5)

> It is a frenzied dance of the mob as it anticipates the tumbrils' doomed passengers on their way to the guillotine.

2. What caused the jury to acquit Charles? (6)

> He renounced his title, came to the aid of Gabelle, married Manette's daughter, and had been tried in England for treason. All of these things were applauded by the jury and audience.

3. How must Miss Pross and Jerry Cruncher perform the household shopping? Why? (7)

> They both had to go to many and various shops to purchase goods so as not to attract attention. Food was scarce in France and large purchases would bring suspicion and resentment.

4. Why is Charles arrested again on the day of his release? (7)

> He has been denounced by the Defarges and also by one other unnamed person.

5. Where does Miss Pross find her brother? (8)

> She bumps into him at a wine shop.

6. Who identifies Solomon Pross as John Barsad? (8)

> Sydney Carton identified him.

7. What does Carton want from Solomon Pross (Barsad)? (8)

> He wants access to the prison, specifically to Charles Darnay should Darnay be sentenced to death.

III (9-11)

1. Why is Mr. Lorry appalled at Cruncher?

> He has learned that Jerry has been a grave-robber.

2. What arrangement has Carton made with Barsad? (9)

> He has assured himself access, only once, to Darnay's cell.

3. Dr. Manette worked to free Darnay during the first imprisonment. Who appears to be quietly working now? (9)
   Carton seems to have taken up the cause.

4. Who is the other person that the court claims has denounced Darnay? (9)
   The court says Dr. Manette has denounced him in his letter.

5. Who is Madame Defarge in Dr. Manette's letter? (10)
   She is the younger sister spoken of in the letter.

6. Why is Charles condemned to die? (10)
   He must pay for the evils of his family, especially his father and uncle.

7. How has Carton changed since he landed in France? (11)
   He stopped drinking and began to act and think for his own ends. He seems stronger, less repugnant to himself, and purposeful.

III (12-15)

1. Where does Madame Defarge plan to end her vengeance? (12)
   She wants total extermination of all aristocrats.

2. Why does Carton have Darnay write the letter? (13)
   He wants Darnay's last letter to be in Darnay's own handwriting.

3. How does Cruncher change? (14)
   He swears never to go "fishing" again or interfere with his wife's "flopping."

4. Why is Miss Pross in a "queer condition"? (14)
   She has killed Madame Defarge and has been deafened by the gun's explosion.

5. Sydney Carton said he would die young because of a dissipated and wasted life. How was he both right and wrong? (15)
   He does die young, but for reasons of love and sacrifice. His death gives him the honor he never attained in life.

6. How is Madame Defarge cheated? (15)
   The one man she wished to see die, more than all others, lives, although without her knowledge, and she cannot reach his wife or child. Her wish for total extermination is not going to come true.

7. What words about the future are attributed to Carton at the end of the novel? (15)
   The words attributed to Carton tell of how he is deeply loved and honored by Charles and Lucie for all of their days, and into their future generations, wherein a boy is given his name and whose son, also his namesake, becomes a great man, one of the most just judges, bringing honor to his name.

MULTIPLE CHOICE STUDY GUIDE/QUIZ QUESTIONS - *A Tale of Two Cities*

I(1-4)

1. Dickens describes England and France in 1775. How does he compare them? (1)
    a. Both are engaged in wars with their colonies.
    b. Both are ruled by kings who enjoy divine right and appear to believe the status quo is unimpeachable and everlasting.
    c. Both are ruled by royal families who are at the end of their lines.
    d. Both governments are on the brink of collapse.

2. Both kings are described as having large jaws; what is Dickens telling us about them? (1)
    a. They are Neanderthal-type men
    b. They share the same family resemblance.
    c. They are stubborn.
    d. They are full of empty talk, stupid and out of touch with the worlds of their subjects.

3. Why are the Dover mail drivers and passengers so apprehensive of each other? (2)
    a. They each think the other may be a government spy.
    b. The mail drivers don't want to carry passengers and the passengers fear the drivers who have been stranding passengers.
    c. They all fear robbery and murder.
    d. The drivers are peasants who resent the aristocratic passengers.

4. How does Dickens describe human beings? (3)
    a. We all have good in us; no one is all bad.
    b. We are an unreliable and greedy bunch.
    c. We are a secret and a mystery to each other.
    d. We are a despicable, wretched race.

5. Explain the meaning of "recalled to life." (4)
    a. A man has been released after 18 years in prison.
    b. A man was revived after being thought dead.
    c. A retired spy was put back into service.
    d. A man who had given up on life met a woman who gave him the will to live.

6. Identify Jarvis Lorry. (4)
    a. He is Lucie Manette's suitor.
    b. He is a gentleman from Tellson's Bank.
    c. He is Mr. Manette's nephew.
    d. He is a government spy pretending to be a banker.

7. Why does Lucie faint upon hearing Mr. Lorry's story? (4)
    a. Mr. Lorry's story is a shock to her.
    b. She is over-tired from traveling.
    c. She is pregnant.
    d. She has become ill.

A Tale of Two Cities Multiple Choice Study Questions Page 2
I (5-6)

1. Dickens uses the broken cask of wine's spilling in the street to foreshadow what future event? (5)
    a. The death of Dr. Manette
    b. The American Revolution
    c. The French Revolution
    d. The death of the kings

2. What is the significance of so many "Jacques" in Defarge's wine shop? (5)
    a. It is just a common name in France--like "Bill" is in America.
    b. It is a common name for a butler, who would be sent to get wine for the family.
    c. It is the common name for "customer" or "friend."
    d. It is a common name for members of the revolution.

3. Who are seen peeping through a hole in the wall at Dr. Manette? (5)
    a. The three Jacques from the wine shop
    b. The police
    c. Government spies
    d. Lucie and Mr. Lorry

4. Why has Defarge allowed them to look in? (5)
    a. The sight will feed the revolution.
    b. He isn't doing anything wrong.
    c. He wants them to see what is going on; it's a plot.
    d. He doesn't realize that they are there.

5. What is Dr. Manette doing when Mr. Lorry and Lucie first see him? (5)
    a. Drinking wine
    b. Making shoes
    c. Just sitting in a corner
    d. Reading

A Tale of Two Cities Multiple Choice Study Questions Page 3

6. Describe Madame Defarge. (6)
    a. Tall, wears furs and jewelry and constantly knits
    b. Small, bony woman who dresses in rags
    c. Dainty, plain, but loud; voices her opinions about everything
    d. Large, robust woman, clearly common

7. What is Dr. Manette's mental state? (6)
    a. He has become a bit forgetful.
    b. His mind is gone; he sits and drools and needs constant care.
    c. He is alert, intelligent, well-spoken and obviously sharp.
    d. His mind has focused on one thing to the exclusion of everything else.

8. Identify One Hundred and Five, North Tower. (6)
    a. Lucie's home address
    b. Dr. Manette's cell number
    c. Meeting place for revolutionists
    d. Address of the wine shop

9. How does Lucie react to Dr. Manette? (6)
    a. She is totally repulsed by him and runs out of the room.
    b. She doesn't recognize him, but she tries to find something familiar.
    c. She dissolves into a mound of tears, her heart broken and her hopes dashed.
    d. She is frightened at first but is quickly overcome with compassion and love.

A Tale of Two Cities Multiple Choice Study Questions Page 4

<u>II (1-4)</u>
1. What does Jerry Cruncher object to his wife doing? (1)
    a. Reading
    b. Drinking
    c. Praying
    d. Going out after dark

2. Who is Charles Darnay? (2)
    a. A young man being tried for treason
    b. One of Dr. Manette's former patients
    c. Lucie's suitor
    d. A man from Tellson's Bank

3. Identify Mr. Stryver. (3)
    a. Dr. Manette's attorney
    b. A leader of the revolution
    c. Darnay's attorney
    d. The prosecutor

4. Who is Mr. Carton? (3)
    a. The prosecutor
    b. Striver's associate
    c. Darnay's attorney
    d. A leader of the revolution

5. Why is Darnay acquitted? (3)
    a. Lack of a positive identification
    b. Lucie's testimony saved him.
    c. Dr. Manette's testimony saved him.
    d. The jury didn't believe Lucie's testimony.

6. How does Mr. Carton feel about himself? (4)
    a. He is egocentric and self-righteous.
    b. He is a disappointment to himself and feels unworthy of love.
    c. He is proud of his achievements and feels good.
    d. He feels guilty because he knows he is a cheater.

A Tale of Two Cities Multiple Choice Study Questions Page 5

II (5-8)
1. What name does Stryver call Carton? (5)
    a. Encyclopedia
    b. Elephant
    c. Memory
    d. Brain

2. What words does Dickens use to describe Stryver and Carton? (5)
    a. Contemptible and Worthless
    b. Stupid and Lazy
    c. Jackass and Mouse
    d. Lion and Jackal

3. What does Carton actually do for Stryver? (5)
    a. Thinking and research
    b. Nothing
    c. Fetches water and meals; butler work
    d. Personal correspondence

4. How does Dickens describe the Manettes' home? (6)
    a. Dark and depressing
    b. Old and stately
    c. Fairytale castle
    d. Sunny and cheery

5. How does Dickens describe the privileged class in France? (7)
    a. Concerned do-gooders
    b. Conservative, intelligent, kind
    c. Self-centered but intelligent and benevolent
    d. Extravagant, superficial and useless

6. What feelings does Monsieur the Marquis have toward the child his carriage has run down?(7)
    a. He hates the child but feels remorseful.
    b. He is very concerned.
    c. None.
    d. He blames the child and the parents who let children run near the coaches.

7. What is the countryside of France like? (8)
    a. The fields have the same starved look that the people do.
    b. The fields are glorious, in contrast with the people.
    c. The fields are neat and clean and colorful.
    d. The countryside is filthy with refuse.

A Tale of Two Cities Multiple Choice Study Questions Page 6

II (9-12)

1. Charles visits his uncle the Marquis and informs him that he renounces his name and property. Why does Charles Darnay do this? (9)
    a. Because he felt guilty
    b. To honor his mother's dying wish
    c. To impress Lucie
    d. To help the revolution

2. In the conversation between the Marquis and Charles, Dickens gives a hint that at one time the Marquis was able to have someone imprisoned. Who? (9)
    a. Charles
    b. Dr. Manette
    c. Lucie
    d. Stryver

3. Why was the Marquis killed? (9)
    a. It was an accident; the mob crushed him
    b. His carriage overturned.
    c. The aristocrats found out he had been helping the common people and the revolution.
    d. The common people rose up against him for running down the child and his careless attitude about the incident.

4. Why doesn't Dr. Manette want Charles to reveal his true name? (10)
    a. He suspects a connection between his past imprisonment and Charles's family.
    b. It would upset Lucie.
    c. He thinks Madame Defarge might find out his true identity.
    d. He doesn't trust Charles.

5. How does Stryver view his marriage to Lucie? (11)
    a. They will live happily ever after, the prince and the princess.
    b. He will marry her for money, but he does not love her.
    c. He will possess a pretty object who will be pleased to marry such a distinguished and gallant gentleman.
    d. He wants to marry her to get revenge for the many wrongs Dr. Manette has done to him.

6. Describe Carton's responses to Stryver's self-flattery. (11)
    a. Carton stabs him with ironic, verbal jabs which completely pass over Stryver's head.
    b. Carton is disgusted and tells Striver so to his face.
    c. Carton is too stupid to see Stryver is an arrogant primadonna and is in awe of Striver.
    d. Carton can't stand Striver any longer. He threatens to leave his employment if Stryver doesn't become less arrogant.

A Tale of Two Cities Multiple Choice Study Questions Page 7

7. How does Stryver react to the certainty that his suit will fail? (12)
    a. He is heart-broken and love-sick.
    b. He congratulates himself that he is rid of a silly, flighty female who will probably come to an impoverished end.
    c. He begins to plot a way to get even with Lucie for rejecting him.
    d. He couldn't care less. he just moves on to the subject of his next conquest and pretends like nothing happened.

A Tale of Two Cities Multiple Choice Study Questions Page 8

II (13-16)

1. What promise does Sydney Carton make to Lucie? (13)
    a. He will destroy Stryver for her.
    b. He will take care of her father.
    c. He would sacrifice himself for those she loves.
    d. He would gladly marry her to help her "save face" in her broken engagement to Stryver.

2. What "fish" does Cruncher go fishing after? (14)
    a. Revolutionaries
    b. Madame Defarge's list of names
    c. Aristocrats
    d. Dead bodies

3. Why are Cruncher's fingers always rusty? (14)
    a. He works in a mine.
    b. He works on a road crew.
    c. he repairs guns for people in the revolution.
    d. He gets them dirty on his fishing trips.

4. Who was the doomed man the road-mender told the Jacques about? (15)
    a. Darnay
    b. Dr. Manette
    c. The man who stabbed the Marquis
    d. Jerry Cruncher

5. What register does Madame Defarge keep? (15)
    a. Names of those who are enemies to the common people
    b. The cash register at the wine shop
    c. The names of the common people who have been tortured and killed
    d. The register of names of the revolutionaries

6. Why does Madame Defarge wear a rose in her hair? (16)
    a. She is an ugly woman trying to look pretty.
    b. The rose is a signal that a spy is in the shop.
    c. She hides secret messages in it for revolutionaries to pick up when they greet her with a hug.
    d. The rose isn't functional. It is Dickens' symbol for the blossoming revolution. The scarlet color is the color of blood shed in the revolution.

A Tale of Two Cities Multiple Choice Study Questions Page 9

7. Why is it ironic that John Barsad should come that particular day? (16)
    a. It is the anniversary of the first day of the revolution.
    b. Madame Defarge is knitting his name into the register.
    c. Charles had just been talking about him with Dr. Manette.
    d. It was the one day that the wine shop was closed.

8. Who else's name is Madame Defarge knitting? (16)
    a. Sydney Carton
    b. Dr. Manette
    c. Stryver
    d. Charles Darnay

A Tale of Two Cities Multiple Choice Study Questions Page 10

II (17-21)

1. Why does Dr. Manette cobble for nine days after Lucie and Charles are married? (18)
    a. It is his way of escaping from distressing news.
    b. Many people have given him work to help him get back into his life again after being in jail for so long.
    c. He is lonesome.
    d. He doesn't have anything else to do.

2. What does Dr. Manette allow Lorry and Miss Pross to do? (19)
    a. Get married
    b. Send a message to Charles for him
    c. Destroy his workbench
    d. Take him out for a "welcome home" feast

3. Why does Lucie ask her husband to speak kindly toward Carton? (20)
    a. She has discovered Carton is Dr. Manette's nephew.
    b. She has seen that he has a good heart and is full of suffering.
    c. Carton will be coming into a fortune when Madame Defarge dies.
    d. He is a spy for Madame Defarge.

4. Lucie's fanciful thought years ago of the echoes of a multitude of footsteps becomes a reality in France. What has occurred? (21)
    a. The mob has destroyed Paris.
    b. The mob has destroyed innocent victims.
    c. The mob has stormed the Bastille in Paris.
    d. The mob has stormed the countryside.

5. What metaphor does Dickens use to describe the mob?
    a. A surging sea
    b. A raging fire
    c. A can of worms
    d. A tornado

6. Who is The Vengeance? (21)
    a. The King's lieutenant
    b. Darnay's cousin
    c. Madame Defarge's lieutenant
    d. A noble woman who has joined the revolution to get even with those who treated her unjustly

A Tale of Two Cities Multiple Choice Study Questions Page 11

II (22-24)

1. Why was grass put in Foulon's mouth? (22)
    a. It was symbolic of the "grass roots" movement of the revolution.
    b. It was the only thing available to keep him quiet.
    c. He had told the starving people to eat grass.
    d. The grass was used to start the fire when the people burned him at the stake.

2. Why does Mr. Lorry have to go to Paris? (24)
    a. He has to get away to try to forget Lucie now that she has married Charles.
    b. Darnay needs him.
    c. He had to leave London quickly and he already had a place to stay in Paris.
    d. He had to go on bank business.

3. Why does Darnay go to France? (24)
    a. To help Gabelle
    b. To help Mr. Lorry
    c. To clear his own name
    d. On a mission for Lucie

4. Why is it foolish of Charles Darnay to go to France? (24)
    a. Dr. Manette and Lucie need him at home.
    b. Madame Defarge has put out a contract on him.
    c. He is a member of the French nobility.
    d. He has no money, no connections, and no chance to help Mr. Lorry anyway.

A Tale of Two Cities Multiple Choice Study Questions Page 12

III (1-4)

1. Why is Charles imprisoned? (1)
    a. He is imprisoned for treason.
    b. He is an emigrant and an aristocrat.
    c. Mr. Lorry framed him, and he got sent to prison. Mr. Lorry got the reward Madame Defarge offered for Darnay.
    d. He is caught helping the revolutionaries.

2. Why does the crowd at the grindstone take up Dr. Manette's cause to free Charles? (2)
    a. Madame Defarge has spread the word that Darnay must be freed.
    b. Dr. Manette is a persuasive speaker and leader. The mob would have followed anyone in their frenzy.
    c. Dr. Manette is a folk hero, so the people support his cause.
    d. This is just another good example of Dickens' use of coincidence.

3. Why does Madame Defarge wish to see Lucie and the younger Lucie? (3)
    a. She wants to remember what they look like so she can register them as she registered all those names in her knitting.
    b. She wants to give them information to warn them about Darnay's secret connections.
    c. She wants to kidnap them to force Darnay to come to her.
    d. She wants to make amends for past wrong-doings.

4. What change has occurred within Dr. Manette? (4)
    a. He has taken up drinking since his cobbler's bench is gone.
    b. He has become morose.
    c. He has sworn revenge on those who took away 18 years of his life and is consumed with hatred.
    d. He has become strong again.

A Tale of Two Cities Multiple Choice Study Questions Page 13

III (5-8)

1. What is the Carmagnole? (5)
    a. A French pub where revolutionaries meet
    b. A frenzied dance of the mob
    c. The name of Defarge's wine shop
    d. Madame Defarge's password

2. What caused the jury to acquit Charles? (6)
    a. He renounced his title.
    b. He came to the aid of Gabelle.
    c. He had been tried in England for treason.
    d. All of the above

3. How must Miss Pross and Jerry Cruncher perform the household shopping? Why? (7)
    a. They have to send out a secret messenger to get the things they need.
    b. They take turns going out in disguise so they will not be recognized.
    c. They call out and goods are delivered.
    d. They both go and make small purchases in many shops.

4. Why is Charles arrested again on the day of his release? (7)
    a. He was denounced by the Defarges and others.
    b. He was only let go so he could be trailed.
    c. Things were very confused during these revolutionary times. The second arrest was a mistake.
    d. He didn't leave the country as he was directed to do.

5. Where does Miss Pross find her brother? (8)
    a. At a cafe
    b. In the Bastille
    c. At a wine shop
    d. In the mob

6. Who identifies Solomon Pross as John Barsad? (8)
    a. Charles Darnay
    b. Sidney Carton
    c. Mr. Lorry
    d. Gabelle

7. What does Carton want from Solomon Pross (Barsad)? (8)
    a. Access to Charles Darnay
    b. A meeting with Madame Defarge
    c. Sage passage to London
    d. Goods for Miss Pross and Jerry Cruncher

A Tale of Two Cities Multiple Choice Study Questions Page 14

<u>III (9-11)</u>

1. Why is Mr. Lorry appalled at Cruncher?
    a. Jerry is planning to kill Madame Defarge.
    b. Jerry has turned in Charles Darnay.
    c. Jerry has been a grave robber.
    d. Jerry thrives on the disquiet the revolution has caused.

2. What arrangement has Carton made with Barsad? (9)
    a. He has arranged to have Madame Defarge murdered.
    b. He has arranged to see Darnay.
    c. He has arranged for an underground hideout.
    d. He has arranged passage for himself and Mr. Lorry to London.

3. Dr. Manette worked to free Darnay during the first imprisonment. Who appears to be quietly working now? (9)
    a. Gabelle
    b. Lucie
    c. Lorry
    d. Carton

4. Who is the other person that the court claims has denounced Darnay? (9)
    a. Dr. Manette
    b. Solomon Press
    c. The Vengeance
    d. Jacques

5. Who is Madame Defarge in Dr. Manette's letter? (10)
    a. The younger sister
    b. The patient
    c. Wife of the Marquis St. Evremonde
    d. Dr. Manette's wife

6. Why is Charles condemned to die? (10)
    a. He killed Madame Defarge's older sister.
    b. He has committed treason.
    c. He must pay for the evils of his family, especially his father and uncle.
    d. His death is just for the new regime to show its power. He is an unlucky victim.

7. How has Carton changed since he landed in France? (11)
    a. Stopped drinking
    b. Began to act and think for himself
    c. Is stronger, less repugnant to himself
    d. All of the above

A Tale of Two Cities Multiple Choice Study Questions Page 15

<u>III (12-15)</u>
1. Where does Madame Defarge plan to end her vengeance? (12)
    a. She doesn't plan to end it.
    b. With the death of Charles Darnay
    c. In Paris
    d. With the total extermination of all aristocrats

2. Why does Carton have Darnay write the letter? (13)
    a. He wants it in Darnay's own handwriting.
    b. He doesn't know what to say.
    c. He can't write.
    d. He wants it to be in Darnay's own words.

3. How does Cruncher change? (14)
    a. He swears never to go fishing again.
    b. He swears to join the priesthood.
    c. He goes crazy.
    d. He becomes sad and quiet.

4. Why is Miss Pross in a "queer condition"? (14)
    a. She is pregnant and unmarried.
    b. She is in a state of shock from Madame Defarge's abuse.
    c. She caught Cruncher "fishing" and became frightened.
    d. She killed Madame Defarge and has been deafened by the gun's explosion.

5. Sydney Carton said he would die young because of a dissipated and wasted life. How was he both right and wrong? (15)
    a. A dissipated and wasted life
    b. Love and sacrifice
    c. Hatred and greed
    d. Accidental suicide

6. How is Madame Defarge cheated? (15)
    a. She never holds an office in the new government.
    b. The register is robbed.
    c. Her wish of total extermination will never come true.
    d. Lucie and Miss Pross escape.

ANSWER KEY - MULTIPLE CHOICE STUDY/QUIZ QUESTIONS
A Tale of Two Cities

I (1-4)	I (5-6)	II (1-4)	II (5-8)
1. B	1. C	1. C	1. C
2. D	2. D	2. A	2. D
3. C	3. A	3. C	3. A
4. C	4. A	4. B	4. D
5. A	5. B	5. A	5. D
6. B	6. A	6. B	6. C
7. C	7. D		7. A
	8. B		
	9. D		

II (9-12)	II (13-16)	II (17-21)	(II 22-24)
1. B	1. C	1. A	1. C
2. B	2. D	2. C	2. D
3. D	3. D	3. B	3. A
4. A	4. C	4. D	4. C
5. C	5. A	5. A	
6. A	6. B	6. C	
7. B	7. B		
	8. D		

III (1-4)	III (5-8)	III (9-11)	III (12-15)
1. B	1. B	1. C	1. D
2. C	2. D	2. B	2. A
3. A	3. D	3. D	3. A
4. D	4. A	4. A	4. D
	5. C	5. A	5. B
	6. B	6. C	6. C
	7. A	7. D	

PREREADING VOCABULARY
WORKSHEETS

VOCABULARY - *A Tale of Two Cities*

I:1-4 Part I: Using Prior Knowledge and Contextual Clues

Below are the sentences in which the vocabulary words appear in the text. Read the sentence. Use any clues you can find in the sentence combined with your prior knowledge, and write what you think the underlined words mean on the lines provided.

1. . . . there were . . . rude carts . . .which the Farmer, Death, had already set apart to be his tumbrils of the Revolution.

_____

2. . . . to entertain any suspicion that they were awake, was to be atheistical and traitorous.

_____

3. . . . one highwayman . . . despoiled the illustrious creature in sight of all his retinue . . .

_____

4. With this hurried adjuration, he cocked his blunderbuss, and stood on the offensive.

_____

5. No more can I look into the depths of this unfathomable water . . . .

_____

6. . . . it is the inexorable consolidation and perpetuation of the secret that was always in that individuality . . . .

_____

7. . . . and a loud watch ticking a sonorous sermon under his flapped waistcoat . . . .

_____

8. I pass my whole life, miss, in turning an immense pecuniary Mangle.

_____

II. Match the correct definitions to the vocabulary words.

___ 1. tumbrils   A. a solemn charge under oath
___ 2. atheistical   B. resonant; loud
___ 3. retinue   C. vehicle carrying condemned persons
___ 4. adjuration   D. unbending; unrelenting
___ 5. unfathomable   E. a train of attendants
___ 6. inexorable   F. not believing in the existence of God
___ 7. sonorous   G. relating to money
___ 8. pecuniary   H. incomprehensible

Vocabulary - *A Tale of Two Cities* I:5-6

Below are the sentences in which the vocabulary words appear in the text. Read the sentence. Use any clues you can find in the sentence combined with your prior knowledge, and write what you think the underlined words mean on the lines provided.

1. The hands of the man who sawed the wood, left red marks on the <u>billets</u>. . . .

_____

2. Hunger . . . started up from the filthy street that had no <u>offal</u> among its refuse, of anything to eat.

_____

3. In his <u>expostulation</u> he dropped his cleaner hand . . . upon the joker's heart.

_____

4. . . . he . . . fell into discourse with the <u>triumvirate</u> of customers who were drinking at the counter.

_____

5. . . . trembling with eagerness to lay the <u>spectral</u> face upon her warm young breast, and love it back to life and hope . . . .

_____

6. Whether he knew what had happened, whether he recollected what they had said to him, whether he knew that he was free, were questions which no <u>sagacity</u> could have solved.

_____

7. . . . no people were <u>discernible</u> at any of the windows . . . .

_____

II. Match the correct definitions to the vocabulary words.

___ 1. billets   A. ghostly
___ 2. offal   B. distinguishable
___ 3. expostulation   C. sticks of wood
___ 4. triumvirate   D. shrewdness; intelligence
___ 5. spectral   E. unusable parts of a butchered animal
___ 6. sagacity   F. coalition of three in office or authority
___ 7. discernible   G. trying to reason with a person

Vocabulary - *A Tale of Two Cities* II (1-4)

Below are the sentences in which the vocabulary words appear in the text. Read the sentence. Use any clues you can find in the sentence combined with your prior knowledge, and write what you think the underlined words mean on the lines provided.

1. Your deeds got into <u>extemporised</u> strong-rooms made of kitchens and sculleries . . . .

_____

2. . . . he had received the added <u>appellation</u> of Jerry.

_____

3. But, the gaol was a vile place, in which most kinds of <u>debauchery</u> and villainy were practised.

_____

4. . . . "Whatever is is right;" an <u>aphorism</u> that would be as final as it is lazy, did it not include the troublesome consequence that nothing that ever was, was wrong.

_____

5. . . . the paleness which his situation <u>engendered</u> came through the brown upon his cheek. . .

_____

6. . . . he . . . was prepared to hear some <u>disparagement</u> attempted of this admirable servant. . .

_____

7. . . . the prisoner already engaged in these <u>pernicious</u> missions. . .

_____

8. . . . on the faith of his solemn <u>asseveration</u> that he already considered the prisoner as good as dead and gone.

_____

9. It clearly being <u>incumbent</u> on some one to say, "Much better."

_____

II. Match the correct definitions to the vocabulary words.
___ 1. extemporised   A. name; title
___ 2. appellation   B. duty or obligation
___ 3. debauchery   C. to be caused or produced
___ 4. aphorism   D. habitual bad conduct
___ 5. engendered   E. spoke without preparation
___ 6. disparagement   F. destructive; deadly
___ 7. pernicious   G. expressed without using many words
___ 8. asseveration   H. serious declaration
___ 9. incumbent   I. comparison to something inferior

Vocabulary - *A Tale of Two Cities* II:5-8

Below are the sentences in which the vocabulary words appear in the text. Read the sentence. Use any clues you can find in the sentence combined with your prior knowledge, and write what you think the underlined words mean on the lines provided.

1. The learned profession of the law was certainly not behind any other learned profession in its Bacchanalian propensities . . . .

   _____

2. With the deprecatory grunt, the jackal again complied.

   _____

3. There ought to have been a tranquil bark in such an anchorage, and there was.

   _____

4. . . . that in the retributive arrangements made by his own hand . . . he stationed Miss Pross much nearer to the lower Angels . . . .

   _____

5. . . . not that I have any fault to find with Doctor Manette, except that he is not worthy of such a daughter, which is no imputation on him, for it was not to be expected that anybody should be . . .

   _____

6. . . . the Chief of them unable to exist with fewer than two gold watches in his pocket, emulative of the noble and chaste fashion set by Monseigneur. . . .

   _____

7. Deep would have been the blot upon his escutcheon if his chocolate had been ignobly waited on by only three men. . .

   _____

8. The sunset struck so brilliantly into the traveling carriage . . . that its occupant was steeped in crimson.

   _____

9. . . . only the difference was, that these faces drooped merely to suffer and not to propitiate .

   _____

Vocabulary - *A Tale of Two Cities* II:5-8 Continued

II. Match the correct definitions to the vocabulary words.

___ 1. Bacchanalian A. soaked
___ 2. deprecatory B. a drunken feast
___ 3. anchorage C. family name, crest, shield
___ 4. imputation D. striving to equal or surpass
___ 5. retributive E. to express regret or disapproval
___ 6. emulative F. atone; make amends
___ 7. escutcheon G. source of reassurance
___ 8. steeped H. punishment given in repayment
___ 9. propitiate I. reproach

Vocabulary - *A Tale of Two Cities* II:9-12

Below are the sentences in which the vocabulary words appear in the text. Read the sentence. Use any clues you can find in the sentence combined with your prior knowledge, and write what you think the underlined words mean on the lines provided.

1. "Good," said the <u>imperturbable</u> master.

_____

2. . . . looked like some enchanted marquis of the <u>impenitently</u> wicked sort . . . .

_____

3. "It is a tone of <u>fervent</u> admiration, true homage, and deep love, Doctor Manette!" he said deferentially.

_____

4. His constraint was so <u>manifest</u>, . . . that Charles Darnay hesitated.

_____

5. . . . the Stryver <u>arrears</u> were handsomely fetched up. . . .

_____

6. As to me--will you never understand that I am <u>incorrigible</u>?

_____

7. . . . Sydney," said Mr. Stryver, preparing him with <u>ostentatious</u> friendliness for the disclosure he was about to make. . . .

_____

8. He was so much too big for Tellson's, that old clerks in distant corners looked up with looks of <u>remonstrance</u>, as though he squeezed them against the wall.

_____

9. Those <u>venerable</u> and feeble persons were always seen by the public in the act of bowing . . .

_____

10. It was a bit of the art of an Old Bailey <u>tactician</u> in which he found great relief.

_____

Vocabulary - *A Tale of Two Cities* II:9-12 Continued

II. Match the correct definitions to the vocabulary words.

___ 1. imperturbable
___ 2. impenitently
___ 3. fervent
___ 4. manifest
___ 5. arrears
___ 6. incorrigible
___ 7. ostentatious
___ 8. remonstrance
___ 9. tactician

A. unfulfilled obligations
B. bad beyond correction or reform
C. with a hardness of heart
D. not movable; calm; can't be bothered
E. evident; obvious
F. strong representation against something
G. earnest
H. skilled in a system or procedure
I. ambitious display

Vocabulary - *A Tale of Two Cities* II: 13-16

Below are the sentences in which the vocabulary words appear in the text. Read the sentence. Use any clues you can find in the sentence combined with your prior knowledge, and write what you think the underlined words mean on the lines provided.

1. But the life I lead, Miss Manette, is not conducive to health. What is to be expected of, or by, such <u>profligates</u>?"

_____

2. The last <u>supplication</u> but one I make to you, is, that you will believe this of me.

_____

3. "I don't know," returned the man, clapping his hands to his mouth nevertheless, and <u>vociferating</u> in a surprising heat and with the greatest ardour, "Spies! Yaha! Tst, tst! Spi-ies!"

_____

4. "Jerry," said Mr. Cruncher, <u>apostrophising</u> himself in his usual way . . . .

_____

5. Thus, Saint Antoine in this <u>vinous</u> feature of his, until midday.

_____

6. Madame Defarge looked <u>superciliously</u> at the client, and nodded in confirmation.

_____

7. Next noontide saw the admirable woman in her usual place in the wine-shop, knitting away <u>assiduously</u>.

_____

II. Match the definitions to the vocabulary words.

___ 1. profligate
___ 2. supplication
___ 3. vociferating
___ 4. apostrophising
___ 5. vinous
___ 6. superciliously
___ 7. assiduously

A. crying out loudly
B. overbearingly; haughtily
C. constantly; diligently
D. showing effects of using wine
E. a depraved man
F. humble begging
G. addressing the absent or dead as if present

Vocabulary - *A Tale of Two Cities* II:17-21

Below are the sentences in which the vocabulary words appear in the text. Read the sentence. Use any clues you can find in the sentence combined with your prior knowledge, and write what you think the underlined words mean on the lines provided.

1. His collected and calm manner could not prevent her blood from running cold, as he thus tried to <u>anatomise</u> his old condition.

_____

2. . . . they had been able to extend it, by taking to themselves the upper rooms formerly belonging to the <u>apocryphal</u> invisible lodger. . .

_____

3. It was not for his friend to <u>abate</u> that confidence.

_____

4. "you see, too," said the Doctor, <u>tremulously</u>, "it is such an old companion."

_____

5. But, Mr. Darnay, <u>oblivion</u> is not so easy to me, as you represent it to be to you.

_____

6. "I would ask you, dearest, to be very generous with him always, and very <u>lenient</u> on his faults when he is not by.

_____

7. Stryver was rich; had married a <u>florid</u> widow with property and three boys . . . .

_____

8. "I know that, to be sure," <u>assented</u> Mr. Lorry, trying to persuade himself that his sweet temper was soured. . . .

_____

9. . . . hard work at neighboring barricades in all directions, shrieks, volleys, <u>execrations</u>, bravery without stint, boom, smash and rattle, and the furious sounding of the living sea . . . .

_____

Vocabulary - *A Tale of Two Cities* II:17-21 Continued

II. Match the correct definitions to the vocabulary words.

___ 1. anatomise   A. highly decorated
___ 2. apocryphal   B. dissect; analyze
___ 3. abate   C. curses
___ 4. tremulously   D. agreed
___ 5. oblivion   E. to lessen
___ 6. lenient   F. trembling; shaking
___ 7. florid   G. state of being forgotten
___ 8. assented   H. indulgent; a mild disposition towards
___ 9. execrations   I. of doubtful authenticity

Vocabulary - *A Tale of Two Cities* II: 22-24

Below are the sentences in which the vocabulary words appear in the text. Read the sentence. Use any clues you can find in the sentence combined with your prior knowledge, and write what you think the underlined words mean on the lines provided.

1. Haggard Saint Antoine had had only one exultant week, in which to soften his <u>modicum</u> of hard and bitter bread to such extent as he could . . .

___

2. The lamps across his streets had a <u>portentously</u> elastic swing with them.

___

3. . . . the powerful frame <u>attenuated</u> by spare living . . .

___

4. A curious <u>contagion</u> of whispering was upon it . . . .

___

5. In the roaring and raging of the <u>conflagration</u>, a red-hot wind, driving straight from the infernal regions, seemed to be blowing the edifice away.

___

6. . . . This, That, and The Other, all had something <u>disparaging</u> to say, in French or in English, concentrating on the Marquis who was not to be found.

___

7. . . . Mr. Stryver shouldered himself into Fleet-street, amidst the general <u>approbation</u> of his hearers . . .

___

II. Match the correct definitions to the vocabulary words.

___ 1. modicum   A. approval; liking
___ 2. portentously   B. a small quantity
___ 3. attenuated   C. infection; diseased by contact
___ 4. contagion   D. dishonorable; inferior
___ 5. conflagration   E. diminished; made thin or slender
___ 6. approbation   F. ominous; foreshadowing something bad
___ 7. disparaging   G. a great fire

Vocabulary - *A Tale of Two Cities* III:1-4

Below are the sentences in which the vocabulary words appear in the text. Read the sentence. Use any clues you can find in the sentence combined with your prior knowledge, and write what you think the underlined words mean on the lines provided.

1. More than enough of bad roads, bad <u>equipages</u> and bad horses . . .

_____

2. . . . their <u>capricious</u> judgement or fancy deemed best for the dawning Republic One and Indivisible, of Liberty, Equality, Fraternity, or Death.

_____

3. Is this the <u>emigrant</u> Evremonde?

_____

4. Monseigneur's house had been first <u>sequestrated</u>, and then confiscated.

_____

5. Defarge looked gloomily at his wife, and gave no other answer than a gruff sound of <u>acquiescence</u>.

_____

6. Beginning to be struck by Defarge's manner, Mr. Lorry looked <u>dubiously</u> at him, and led the way.

_____

7. . . . that the prisoner must remain in custody, but should, for his sake, be held <u>inviolate</u> in safe custody.

_____

II. Match the correct definitions to the vocabulary words.

   ___ 1. equipages   A. uninjured; unbroken
   ___ 2. capricious   B. taking custody of a defendant's property
   ___ 3. emigrant   C. equipment
   ___ 4. sequestrated   D. whimsical
   ___ 5. acquiescence   E. uncertain; doubtful
   ___ 6. dubiously   F. compliance
   ___ 7. inviolate   G. one who moved residence from one country
                                        to another

Vocabulary - *A Tale of Two Cities* III:5-8

Below are the sentences in which the vocabulary words appear in the text. Read the sentence. Use any clues you can find in the sentence combined with your prior knowledge, and write what you think the underlined words mean on the lines provided.

1. As soon as they were established in their new residence, and her father had entered on the routine of his <u>avocations</u> . . . .

_____

2. The wood-sawyer, who was a little man with a <u>redundancy</u> of gesture . . . .

_____

3. Miss Pross and Mr. Cruncher had discharged the office of <u>purveyors</u>, the former carrying the money; the latter, the basket.

_____

4. "Hush, dear! Again?" Lucie <u>remonstrated</u>.

_____

5. As if the estrangement between them had come of any <u>culpability</u> of her.

_____

6. The smooth manner of the spy, curiously in <u>dissonance</u> with his ostentatiously rough dress . . .

_____

II. Match the correct definitions to the vocabulary words.

___ 1. avocations   A. those who supply provisions
___ 2. redundancy   B. guilt; sinfulness; responsibility
___ 3. purveyors   C. occupations
___ 4. remonstrated   D. discord; disagreement in sound
___ 5. culpability   E. using or having more than necessary
___ 6. dissonance   F. presented strong reasons against
                                            something

Vocabulary - *A Tale of Two Cities* III:9-11

Below are the sentences in which the vocabulary words appear in the text. Read the sentence. Use any clues you can find in the sentence combined with your prior knowledge, and write what you think the underlined words mean on the lines provided.

1. "Now, what I would humbly offer to you, sir," pursued Mr. Cruncher, "even if it was so, which I don't say it is--" Don't prevaricate," said Mr. Lorry.

___

2. Suspected and Denounced enemy of the Republic, Aristocrat, one of a family of tyrants, one of a race proscribed for that they had used their abolished privileges to the infamous oppression of the people, Charles Evremonde, called Darnay, in right of such proscription, absolutely Dead in Law.

___

3. The manner of both was imperious, and they both moved as these words were spoken, so as to place me between themselves and the carriage door. They were armed. I was not.

___

4. There is prodigious strength . . . in sorrow and despair.

___

5. We know now, the natural antipathy you strove against, and conquered, for her dear sake.

___

II. Match the correct definitions to the vocabulary words.

___ 1. prevaricate   A. dislike; opposition
___ 2. proscribed   B. extraordinary; huge
___ 3. imperious   C. to act or speak evasively
___ 4. prodigious   D. haughty; arrogant; domineering
___ 5. antipathy   E. outlawed; condemned as dangerous

Vocabulary - *A Tale of Two Cities* III:12-15

Below are the sentences in which the vocabulary words appear in the text. Read the sentence. Use any clues you can find in the sentence combined with your prior knowledge, and write what you think the underlined words mean on the lines provided.

1. Suddenly, the positions exchange speech with animated <u>gesticulation</u>, and the horses are pulled up, almost on their haunches.

_____

2. Ogre that he was, he spoke like an <u>epicure</u>.

_____

3. "I willingly obey the orders of my Chief," said The Vengeance with <u>alacrity</u>, and kissing her cheek.

_____

4. But, imbued from her childhood with a brooding sense of wrong, and an <u>inveterate</u> hatred of a class, opportunity had developed her into a tigress.

_____

5. Lying hidden at her waist, was a sharpened dagger. Thus <u>accoutred</u>, and walking with the confident tread of such a character . . . Madame Defarge took her way along the streets.

_____

6. Sow the same seed of <u>rapacious</u> license and oppression over again, and it will surely yield the same fruit according to its kind.

_____

7. I see the evil of this time and of the previous time of which this is the natural birth, gradually making <u>expiation</u> for itself and wearing out.

_____

II. Match the correct definitions to the vocabulary words.

___ 1. gesticulation   A. liveliness; cheerful readiness
___ 2. epicure   B. atonement; reparation
___ 3. alacrity   C. to make motions while talking
___ 4. inveterate   D. subsisting on prey; plundering
___ 5. accoutred   E. long-established; deep-rooted
___ 6. rapacious   F. devoted to sensual enjoyments
___ 7. expiation   G. furnished with military dress & arms

KEY - VOCABULARY
A Tale of Two Cities

I (1-4)
1. C
2. F
3. E
4. A
5. H
6. D
7. B
8. G

I (5-6)
1. C
2. E
3. G
4. F
5. A
6. D
7. B

II (1-4)
1. E
2. A
3. D
4. G
5. C
6. I
7. F
8. H
9. B

II (5-8)
1. B
2. E
3. G
4. I
5. H
6. D
7. C
8. A
9. F

II (9-12)
1. D
2. C
3. G
4. E
5. A
6. B
7. I
8. F
9. H

II (13-16)
1. E
2. F
3. A
4. G
5. D
6. B
7. C

II (17-21)
1. B
2. I
3. E
4. F
5. G
6. H
7. A
8. D
9. C

(II 22-24)
1. B
2. F
3. E
4. C
5. G
6. A
7. D

III (1-4)
1. C
2. D
3. G
4. B
5. F
6. E
7. A

III (5-8)
1. C
2. E
3. A
4. F
5. B
6. D

III (9-11)
1. C
2. E
3. D
4. B
5. A

III (12-15)
1. C
2. F
3. A
4. E
5. G
6 D
7. B

DAILY LESSONS

LESSON ONE

Objectives
    1. To introduce the *A Tale of Two Cities* unit.
    2. To distribute books and other related materials (study guides, reading assignments, etc.).
    3. To preview the study questions for chapters 1-3
    4. To familiarize students with the vocabulary for chapters 1-3

NOTE: For this unit, if possible, divide your classroom into two halves. Separate students' desks so it is obvious that they are in two distinct groups. One side of your room and half of your students will be English/Londoners. The other side of your room and the other half of your students will be French/Parisians. If you have room, decorate each side of your room to match: make one side English and one side French. Some graphics are included with this unit to help you.

Activity #1
    Post a list on your board or overhead projector telling students whether they are French or English so they know on which side of the room to sit when they come into class.
    Explain to students that they are about to embark on a "Tale of Two Cities" during which they will read a story which links the two cities of London and Paris and also during which they, the students, will temporarily have a change of nationality. While they are reading the story *A Tale of Two Cities* by Charles Dickens, they will also be telling a tale of two cities on fantastic, whirlwind tours of London and Paris.

Activity #2
    Have students in each group get together for about five minutes to brainstorm everything they know about their respective cities. After students have created their lists, have one student from each group read the lists.

TRANSITION: Tell students that in a couple of days they will be getting their specific project assignments. For now, it is time to pull out the main materials they will need for this unit, time to get the first *Tale of Two Cities* underway.

Activity #3
    Distribute the materials students will use in this unit. Explain in detail how students are to use these materials.

    <u>Study Guides</u> Students should read the study guide questions for each reading assignment prior to beginning the reading assignment to get a feeling for what events and ideas are important in the section they are about to read. After reading the section, students will (as a class or individually) answer the questions to review the important events and ideas from that section of the book. Students should keep the study guides as study materials for the unit test.

<u>Vocabulary</u>   Prior to reading a reading assignment, students will do vocabulary work related to the section of the book they are about to read. Following the completion of the reading of the book, there will be a vocabulary review of all the words used in the vocabulary assignments. Students should keep their vocabulary work as study materials for the unit test.

<u>Reading Assignment Sheet</u>   You (the teachers) need to fill in the reading assignment sheet to let students know by when their reading has to be completed. You can either write the assignment sheet up on a side blackboard or bulletinboard and leave it there for students to see each day, or you can "ditto" copies for each student to have. In either case, you should advise students to become very familiar with the reading assignments so they know what is expected of them.

<u>Extra Activities Center</u>   The Extra Activities Packet portion of this unit contains suggestions for an extra library of related books and articles in your classroom as well as crossword and word search puzzles. Make an extra activities center in your room where you will keep these materials for students to use. (Bring the books and articles in from the library and keep several copies of the puzzles on hand.) Explain to students that these materials are available for students to use when they finish reading assignments or other class work early.

<u>Books</u>   Each school has its own rules and regulations regarding student use of school books. Advise students of the procedures that are normal for your school.

<u>Activity #4</u>
Preview the study questions and have students do the vocabulary work for I(1-4) of *A Tale of Two Cities*. (This will be referred to as "the prereading work" throughout this unit.) If students do not finish this assignment during this class period, they should complete it prior to the next class meeting.

LESSON TWO

Objectives
1. To read I(1-4)
2. To give students practice reading orally
3. To evaluate students' oral reading
4. To do the prereading work for I(5-6)

Activity #1

Have students read I(1-4) of *A Tale of Two Cities* out loud in class. You probably know the best way to get readers with your class; pick students at random, ask for volunteers, or use whatever method works best for your group. If you have not yet completed an oral reading evaluation for your students this marking period, this would be a good opportunity to do so. A form is included with this unit for your convenience.

If students do not complete this reading assignment in class, they should do so prior to your next class meeting.

Activity #2

Tell students that prior to your next class period they should have completed the prereading work for I(5-6).

LESSON THREE

Objectives
1. To review the main events and ideas from I(1-4)
2. To read I(5-6)
3. To complete the oral reading evaluations

Activity #1

Give students a few minutes to formulate answers for the study guide questions for I(1-4), and then discuss the answers to the questions in detail. Write the answers on the board or overhead transparency so students can have the correct answers for study purposes. Note: It is a good practice in public speaking and leadership skills for individual students to take charge of leading the discussions of the study questions. Perhaps a different student could go to the front of the class and lead the discussion each day that the study questions are discussed during this unit. Of course, the teacher should guide the discussion when appropriate and be sure to fill in any gaps the students leave.

Activity #2

Have students read I(5-6) of *A Tale of Two Cities* orally in class. Complete the oral reading evaluations if you have not yet done so. If students do not complete this reading assignment in class, they should do so prior to your next class period.

Activity #3

Tell students that prior to your next class period they should complete the prereading work for II(1-4).

ORAL READING EVALUATION

Name _____ Class____ Date _____

SKILL	EXCELLENT	GOOD	AVERAGE	FAIR	POOR
Fluency	5	4	3	2	1
Clarity	5	4	3	2	1
Audibility	5	4	3	2	1
Pronunciation	5	4	3	2	1
_____	5	4	3	2	1
_____	5	4	3	2	1

Total _____   Grade _____

Comments:

LESSON FOUR

Objectives
    1. To review the main ideas and events from I(5-6)
    2. To make the project assignment and give students some time to get started on it
    3. To do the prereading work for II(1-4)

Activity #1

    Give students a few minutes to formulate answers for the study guide questions for I(5-6), and then discuss the answers to the questions in detail. Write the answers on the board or overhead transparency so students can have the correct answers for study purposes.

Activity #2

    Distribute the Project Assignment Sheets and Writing Assignment #1. Discuss the directions in detail and give students the remainder of the class period to begin working on this assignment.

NOTE: You need to fill in the dates that the project presentations are due and the order in which they are due.
    Suggested order is: London Society Page, Paris Society Page, London Tour Bus, Paris Tour Bus, London Time Capsule/Newsreel, Paris Time Capsule/Newsreel. This order gives students doing similar tasks approximately the same amount of time to complete the tasks. It also gives those who may need a few extra days to do videotape editing a little extra time to get that done.
    An alternate order is: London Time Capsule/Newsreel, London Tour Bus, London Society Page, Paris Time Capsule/Newsreel, Paris Tour Bus, Paris Society Page. This order presents all the information about one city in a relatively logical order before proceeding to the next city.

Activity #3

    Tell students that prior to your next class period they should read II(1-4).

PROJECT ASSIGNMENT SHEET - *A Tale of Two Cities*

PURPOSE

The purpose of this assignment is to explore the history, current events, culture and sights of two historically important and wonderful European cities to enrich your understanding of the novel *A Tale of Two Cities* and to enrich your understanding of your world.

DESCRIPTION

The end result of this project will be the creation of six different group, multi-media presentations, three presentations from the Londoners and three presentations from the Parisians. Following the oral, multi-media presentations, each group member will be responsible for handing in a written summary of the research he/she did to contribute to the presentations. (That will be Writing Assignment #1, an informative composition.)

DETAILS

You are already divided into two large groups: those of you who are Londoners and those of you who are Parisians. In your first town meetings, you will divide yourselves into three smaller groups. There will then be three groups of Londoners and three groups of Parisians.

Group One: "Time Capsule/Newsreel"

Your job is to fill us in on the history of your city and bring us to date with current events in your fine town. You are called "Time Capsule/Newsreel" because this is how you are to make your presentations. The historical portion is to be done like a time capsule. You are to carefully choose pictures and/or objects which each represent a key event in the history of your city. The pictures may be photos (big enough for everyone to see), drawings, video or television pictures, paintings, etc. As you show the picture or object, you are to give a brief description of its relevance. The current events portion is to be done like a newsreel. You may video reporters "live" from some appropriate scene in London. You may use actual videotaped newsreel footage. You may do your report "live" without videotape. The reports you choose to do must focus on key issues of current events in London.

Group Two: "Society Page"

Your job is to give us the scoop from the social scene in your city. We want to know about the arts, food, entertainment, customs, holidays, language (Let's hear those wonderful English and French accents!), and things that are "typically French" or "typically English." Your presentations should take many different forms. We'll expect to have a taste of some of your city's favorite recipes, hear some of your finest traditional music, see pictures or videos about your entertainment, customs and holidays. A real-life fashion show would be fun. Use your imagination to bring your topics to life!

Tale of Two Cities Project Assignment Page 2

    Group Three: "Tour Bus"
        This title is pretty self-explanatory. Your job is to take us on a guided tour of your city. We want to see and know about all the most famous and important sights. It would also be nice to know how much we're going to have to pay to stay in your fine city for a little vacation (hotel rates, general prices of food, admissions, transportation, etc.). Use pictures, videos, maps, slides and any other visual aides you can find to give us the full effect of having visited your city. (By-the-way, where can we get a good cup of coffee and a delicious dinner? A few notes about restaurants would be helpful!)

TIME
    You need to get started quickly. You don't have a lot of time to waste. Your tales of your two cities, your presentations, will be due on the following schedule:

    _____ Presentation 1: _____
    _____ Presentation 2: _____
    _____ Presentation 3: _____
    _____ Presentation 4: _____
    _____ Presentation 5: _____
    _____ Presentation 6: _____

    You will have one class period for general planning, one class period in the library, and one class period after going to the library to work on your presentations. You will need to make arrangements to do a portion of the work for this project after class hours.

GETTING STARTED
    Hold a town meeting and divide yourselves up into three groups: Time Capsule/Newsreel, Society Page, and Tour Bus.
    Meet with the members of your small group to brainstorm (and jot down) ideas you have for your project. Decide what needs to be done and try to find ways do divide up the tasks that need to be done so your work can be done quickly and efficiently.
    First, you probably need to find information. Make a list of the information you need to find and the specific places you need to look to try to find it. Divide the list contents among the group members.
    You are scheduled to go to the library. After you gather the materials you need from there, divide up the reading or viewing. Have all group members do their research and then report back to the group at another group meeting. At this meeting, decide upon the specific presentation form for each bit of information. Divide the presentation preparation up among the group members and make any other necessary arrangements.

Tale of Two Cities Project Assignment Page 3

SUGGESTIONS

Time Capsule/Newsreel

Contact your local television news department to see if they have any fairly recent, videotaped stories about London/Paris you could borrow or have a copy of. Check with a local museum for any articles the curator or his representative might be willing to bring to your presentation. Check with your local newspaper office to find out where you could get a copy of a recent newspaper from London/Paris. Perhaps someone could fax you some of the top stories if you can't actually get the paper.

Society Page

Cookbooks, magazines, high fashion boutiques, record stores & library media centers, and genealogical societies (often know a lot about customs) will be some of your best bets for extra materials (besides the library).

Tour Bus

Your best source of extra materials will probably be a travel agency. Call several of your local travel agencies, explain that you are doing a project for school and explain the types of materials and information you will need. Ask if they have anything that might help you. Some of the larger video rental stores have sections of travel videos; you might also check there for additional help.

WRITING ASSIGNMENT #1 - *A Tale of Two Cities*

PROMPT
Each person in your group is responsible for a portion of the research that needs to be done in conjunction with your projects. The purpose of this composition is for you to summarize the information you gathered and tell what you did for the project.

PREWRITING
Gather the notes you took as you did your research. On a piece of paper, jot down everything you did to work on this project.

DRAFTING
This composition is to be done in a report format rather than as an essay. You will have a heading at the top of the first page stating your name, class, group, and the date. Your composition will be divided into two main sections: a section to tell what you actually did to contribute to your group's project and a section for factual information you gathered.

First make a heading that says <u>MY CONTRIBUTION</u>. Under that heading write one or several paragraphs (depending on how much you did) in which you tell what you did for the project. Include trips to the library, phone calls, stops at stores--everything you did related to this project.

Next, make a heading that says <u>MY RESEARCH</u>. Under this heading you will have several smaller headings, one for each bit of research you did. For example, if you read a magazine article called "French Cooking," make a heading that says <u>"French Cooking" an article in *Cooking Digest*</u>. If you viewed a videotape called "The Sights and Sounds of London," make a heading that says <u>"The Sights and Sounds of London," a video</u>. Make one of these headings for each thing you read or saw to gather information. Under these headings, write a short summary of the information you found.

PROMPT
When you finish the rough draft of your paper, ask a student who sits near you to read it. After reading your rough draft, he/she should tell you what he/she liked best about your work, which parts were difficult to understand, and ways in which your work could be improved. Reread your paper considering your critic's comments, and make the corrections you think are necessary.

PROOFREADING
Do a final proofreading of your paper double-checking your grammar, spelling, organization, and the clarity of your ideas.

LESSON FIVE

Objectives
    1. To review the main ideas and events of II(1-4)
    2. To preview and read II(5-8)
    3. To give students time to work on their research projects

Activity #1
    Distribute quizzes for II(1-4). Use the multiple choice study questions for this section of the book (or if your students usually use the multiple choice questions, use the short answer version for your quiz). Give students a few minutes to answer the questions, then have students exchange papers and grade the quizzes. (A great deal of the reading of this novel is done out of the classroom, so it is important that students take the home reading assignments seriously. By having a quiz in this class period, you alert the students to the fact that there may be other quizzes and theoretically improve the probability that the reading assignments will be done on time.)

Activity #2
    Tell students that prior to your next class period they should do the prereading work and read II(5-8).

Activity #3
    Take students to the library and give them the remainder of the class time to work on their research projects.

LESSON SIX

Objectives
    1. To review the main ideas and events from II(5-8)
    2. To do the prereading work for II(9-12)
    3. To read II(9-12)

Activity #1
    Give students a few minutes to formulate answers for the study guide questions for II(5-8), and then discuss the answers to the questions in detail. Write the answers on the board or overhead transparency so students can have the correct answers for study purposes.

Activity #2
    Tell students that prior to your next class period they must have done the prereading work for and have read II(9-12). Give students the remainder of this class period to do this assignment.

LESSON SEVEN

Objectives
    1. To review the main ideas from II(9-12)
    2. To preview the study questions for II(13-16)
    3. To read II(13-16)
    4. To give students time to work on their research projects

Activity #1
    Give students a few minutes to formulate answers for the study guide questions for II(9-12), and then discuss the answers to the questions in detail. Write the answers on the board or overhead transparency so students can have the correct answers for study purposes.

Activity #2
    Tell students that prior to your next class period they must have done the prereading work for and have read II(13-16).

Activity #3
    Give students the remainder of this class period to work on their research projects.

LESSON EIGHT

Objectives
    1. To review the main events and ideas from II(13-16)
    2. To preview and read II(17-21)
    3. To give students the opportunity to practice writing to express their own personal opinions
    4. To give the teacher the opportunity to evaluate students' writing
    5. To get students to think and form an opinion about their own neighborhoods

Activity #1
    Give students a few minutes to formulate answers for the study guide questions for II(13-16), and then discuss the answers to the questions in detail. Write the answers on the board or overhead transparency so students can have the correct answers for study purposes.

Activity #2
    Tell students that prior to your next class period they must have done the prereading work for and have read II(17-21).

Activity #3
    Distribute Writing Assignment #2. Discuss the directions in detail and give students the remainder of this class period to work on it. Note: Because the choice of assignments is so wide, it was not possible to include the usual PREWRITNG and DRAFTING sections on the writing assignment sheet.

WRITING ASSIGNMENT #2 - *A Tale of Two Cities*

PROMPT

What do you think of the place where you live -- your city or town? In this assignment, you are to express your personal opinions about the place where you live. The structure of the assignment is up to you. Here are some suggestions:

1. Tell about something that has happened in your city or town that has affected you personally. Explain what happened and how it affected you.

2. Pick an incident that has happened in your city that is a great example that shows just what you think of your city or town. Explain the incident's relevance to your thoughts.

3. Choose a neighborhood that you think is typical of your city or town. Describe it and tell why it is typical of your city or town.

4. Write a short story or play. Through the characters show your point of view about your city or town.

5. Make a narrated video of your city or town to give to your local travel or real estate agency to show people who are interested in moving to your area. If you choose this option, use this class time to decide which things in your city/town you will show in your video and in what order you will show them. Write out the script for the narration.

Choose ONE of the above assignments.

PROMPT

When you finish the rough draft of your paper, ask a student who sits near you to read it. After reading your rough draft, he/she should tell you what he/she liked best about your work, which parts were difficult to understand, and ways in which your work could be improved. Reread your paper considering your critic's comments, and make the corrections you think are necessary.

PROOFREADING

Do a final proofreading of your paper double-checking your grammar, spelling, organization, and the clarity of your ideas.

LESSON NINE

Objectives
    1. To review the main events and ideas from II(17-21)
    2. To preview and read II(22-24)

Activity #1
    Give students a few minutes to formulate answers for the study guide questions for II(17-21), and then discuss the answers to the questions in detail. Write the answers on the board or overhead transparency so students can have the correct answers for study purposes.

Activity #2
    Tell students that prior to your next class period they must have done the prereading work for and have read II(22-24). Give students the remainder of this class period to work on this assignment.

LESSON TEN

Objectives
    1. To review the main events and ideas from II(22-24)
    2. To preview and read III(1-4)
    3. To view and evaluate Group Presentation 1

Activity #1
    Give students a few minutes to formulate answers for the study guide questions for II(22-24), and then discuss the answers to the questions in detail. Write the answers on the board or overhead transparency so students can have the correct answers for study purposes.

Activity #2
    Tell students that prior to your next class period they must have done the prereading work for and have read III(1-4).

Activity #3
    Use the remainder of this class period to view and evaluate Group Presentation 1. An evaluation form is included with this unit for your convenience.

NOTE: This evaluation form is to evaluate the group presentation. Evaluation of individual participation will be done through Writing Assignment #1.

GROUP PRESENTATION EVALUATION FORM
A Tale of Two Cities

Group Presentation # ___   Class _____   Date _____

Group Members

_____   _____   _____

_____   _____   _____

_____   _____   _____

Grading Scale: 10 is excellent to 1 which is very poor

____ Were the topics assigned thoroughly covered? _____

____ Was it a multi-media presentation? _____

____ Was it organized? _____

____ Was it clear--easy to understand? _____

____ Was it presented with enthusiasm? _____

____ Was it easily visible and easily heard? _____

____ (other)

____ (other)

____ (other)

____ TOTAL POINTS out of a possible _____

COMMENTS:

LESSON ELEVEN

Objectives
- 1. To review the main events and ideas from III(1-4)
- 2. To preview and read III(5-8)
- 3. To view and evaluate Group Presentation 2

Activity #1
    Give students a few minutes to formulate answers for the study guide questions for III(1-4), and then discuss the answers to the questions in detail. Write the answers on the board or overhead transparency so students can have the correct answers for study purposes.

Activity #2
    Tell students that prior to your next class period they must have done the prereading work for and have read III(5-8).

Activity #3
    Use the remainder of this class period to view and evaluate Group Presentation 2.

LESSON TWELVE

Objectives
- 1. To review the main events and ideas from III(5-8)
- 2. To preview and read III(9-11)
- 3. To view and evaluate Group Presentation 3

Activity #1
    Give students a few minutes to formulate answers for the study guide questions for III(5-8), and then discuss the answers to the questions in detail. Write the answers on the board or overhead transparency so students can have the correct answers for study purposes.

Activity #2
    Tell students that prior to your next class period they must have done the prereading work for and have read III(9-11).

Activity #3
    Use the remainder of this class period to view and evaluate Group Presentation 3.

LESSON THIRTEEN

Objectives
1. To review the main events and ideas from III(9-11)
2. To preview and read III(12-15)
3. To view and evaluate Group Presentation 4

Activity #1
Give students a few minutes to formulate answers for the study guide questions for III(9-11), and then discuss the answers to the questions in detail. Write the answers on the board or overhead transparency so students can have the correct answers for study purposes.

Activity #2
Tell students that prior to your next class period they must have done the prereading work for and have read III(12-15).

Activity #3
Use the remainder of this class period to view and evaluate Group Presentation 4.

LESSON FOURTEEN

Objectives
1. To review the main events and ideas from III(12-15)
2. To view and evaluate Group Presentation 5

Activity #1
Give students a few minutes to formulate answers for the study guide questions for III(12-15), and then discuss the answers to the questions in detail. Write the answers on the board or overhead transparency so students can have the correct answers for study purposes.

Activity #2
Use the remainder of this class period to view and evaluate Group Presentation 5.

LESSON FIFTEEN

Objective
1. To view and evaluate Group Presentation 6
2. To make final evaluations and comments about the Group Presentations

Activity
Use this class period to view and evaluate Group Presentation 6 and to make any final comments you may have about the quality of the projects and enthusiasm with which they were prepared and presented.

LESSON SIXTEEN

Objective
> To review all of the vocabulary work done in this unit

Activity
> Choose one (or more) of the vocabulary review activities listed below and spend your class period as directed in the activity. Some of the materials for these review activities are located in the Extra Activities Packet in this unit.

VOCABULARY REVIEW ACTIVITIES

1. Divide your class into two teams and have an old-fashioned spelling or definition bee.

2. Give each of your students (or students in groups of two, three or four) a *Tale of Two Cities* Vocabulary Word Search Puzzle. The person (group) to find all of the vocabulary words in the puzzle first wins.

3. Give students *A Tale of Two Cities* Vocabulary Word Search Puzzle without the word list. The person or group to find the most vocabulary words in the puzzle wins.

4. Use *Tale of Two Cities* Vocabulary Crossword Puzzle. Put the puzzle onto a transparency on the overhead projector (so everyone can see it), and do the puzzle together as a class.

5. Give students *A Tale of Two Cities* Vocabulary Matching Worksheet to do.

6. Divide your class into two teams. Use the *A Tale of Two Cities* vocabulary words with their letters jumbled as a word list. Student 1 from Team A faces off against Student 1 from Team B. You write the first jumbled word on the board. The first student (1A or 1B) to unscramble the word wins the chance for his/her team to score points. If 1A wins the jumble, go to student 2A and give him/her a definition. He/she must give you the correct spelling of the vocabulary word which fits that definition. If he/she does, Team A scores a point, and you give student 3A a definition for which you expect a correctly spelled matching vocabulary word. Continue giving Team A definitions until some team member makes an incorrect response. An incorrect response sends the game back to the jumbled-word face off, this time with students 2A and 2B. Instead of repeating giving definitions to the first few students of each team, continue with the student after the one who gave the last incorrect response on the team. For example, if Team B wins the jumbled-word face-off, and student 5B gave the last incorrect answer for Team B, you would start this round of definition questions with student 6B, and so on. The team with the most points wins!

7. Have students write a story in which they correctly use as many vocabulary words as possible. Have students read their compositions orally! Post the most original compositions on your bulletin board!

LESSON SEVENTEEN

Objectives
    1. To discuss major themes, ideas and narrative techniques of A Tale Of Two Cities
    2. To give students the opportunity to practice their group interaction skills

Activity #1
    Divide your class into 9 groups - one group for each of the following topics:
        1. Manette family relationships with Evremonde family
        2. Compare/contrast Paris and London
        3. Animal imagery
        4. Lucie as "good" vs Madame Defarge as "evil"
        5. Mobs
        6. Coincidence
        7. Death vs life; "recalled to life"
        8. Aristocrats/nobility vs common people/revolutionaries
        9. The organization of the novel

    Each group should prepare to "teach" its topic to the class. Each group should find specific examples from the text to show and support the points made about the topic. Having one group member as a "secretary" to jot down the group's thoughts and specific examples will help. The secretary should also be the spokesperson (since he or she will be able to decipher the notes taken).

    NOTE Feel free to add to or subtract from the topics listed above, depending on the level of your students. These are some basic ideas.

Activity #3
    Ask each group's spokesperson to give the group's thoughts about the topic. Jot these down on the board or overhead projector and use them as a springboard for a discussion of the topics.

LESSON EIGHTEEN

Objectives
    1. To complete the discussions begun in Lesson Seventeen
    2. To continue discussing *A Tale of Two Cities* on the interpretive and critical levels

Activity #1
    Complete any discussions left-over from Lesson Seventeen.

Activity #2
    Choose the questions from the Extra Discussion Questions/Writing Assignments which seem most appropriate for your students. A class discussion of these questions is most effective if students have been given the opportunity to formulate answers to the questions prior to the discussion. To this end, you may either have all the students formulate answers to all the questions, divide your class into groups and assign one or more questions to each group, or you could assign one question to each student in your class. The option you choose will make a difference in the amount of class time needed for this activity.

Activity #3

    After students have had ample time to formulate answers to the questions, begin your class discussion of the questions and the ideas presented by the questions. Be sure students take notes during the discussion so they have information to study for the unit test.

EXTRA WRITING ASSIGNMENTS/DISCUSSION QUESTIONS
A Tale of Two Cities

Interpretation

1. From what point of view is the story told? Why is that important?

2. Charles Dickens is well-known for his life-like characters. Explain how he uses them to add meaning to *A Tale of Two Cities*.

3. Where is the climax of the story? Defend your choice.

4. Explain the importance of the settings in *A Tale of Two Cities*. Could the same story have been told in another place and time and still have had the same effect?

5. In what ways does Charles Dickens try to make the story believable? Is he successful; is it believable?

6. What are the main conflicts in the story and how are they resolved?

7. Characterize Charles Dickens's style and explain how it affects our perception of his work.

8. In what ways is *A Tale of Two Cities* a mystery story?

Critical

9. Explain how in *A Tale of Two Cities* "future" generations are affected by the past.

10. Analyze Dickens's use of Tellson's Bank as a prison.

11. Explain the use and importance of knitting and cobbling.

12. Explain the first paragraph of the story.

13. Compare and contrast Charles Darnay with his father and uncle.

14. Explain the roles of these characters in the story: Barsad, Cruncher, Gabelle, Mr. Lorry, Marquis de St. Evermonde, and Stryver. How was each of these characters important?

15. Why did Dickens choose to call this book *A Tale of Two Cities* instead of *Aristocrats and Peasants*, for example?

16. Categorize the following characters as "good guys" or "bad guys": Madame Defarge, Marquis de St. Evermonde, Stryver, Cruncher, Dr. Manette, Charles Darnay, Barsad (Solomon Pross), Cly and Carton.

Tale of Two Cities Extra Discussion Questions/Writing Assignments Page 2

17. Compare and contrast Stryver and Carton.

18. Discuss Dickens's use of coincidence in *A Tale of Two Cities*.

19. Discuss Dickens's use of symbolism in *A Tale of Two Cities*.

20. What are the main themes/ideas presented in *A Tale of Two Cities*?

21. What is Lucie's use as a character? Would the story have essentially been the same without her? Why or why not? Why was she included?

Critical/Personal Response
22. Suppose the story had been written in the first person narrative by Charles Darnay. How would that have affected our perception of the events?

23. Is there enough information about the French Revolution in this story to classify the book as "historical fiction"? Why or why not?

24. Suppose Darnay had been sent to the guillotine at the end of the story. How would the messages of the book have changed?

25. What kind of a book is *A Tale of Two Cities*? A tragedy? A romance? A gothic novel? Historical fiction? Science fiction? What?

Personal Response
26. If you could have been any character in this book, which one would you have liked to have been?

27. Did you enjoy reading *A Tale of Two Cities*? Why or why not?

28. The French Revolution was a noteworthy revolution from the past. What are some more recent revolutions that have occurred in the world?

29. What, actually, is an aristocrat? Are they all bad?

30. Does this book have a hero? If so, who is it? If not, why doesn't anyone qualify to be called a "hero"?

LESSON NINETEEN

Objectives
    1. To give students the opportunity to practice writing to persuade
    2. To have students take a look at their own towns/cities
    3. To review the information about Paris and London
    4. To have students analyze information, make a determination about it, and communicate that determination
    5. To give the teacher the opportunity to evaluate students' writing skills

Activity
    Distribute Writing Assignment #3. Discuss the directions in detail and give students ample time to complete the assignment. Be sure to tell students when their assignments have to be handed in for grading.

LESSON TWENTY

Objectives
    1. To review the main ideas presented in *A Tale of Two Cities*
    2. To discuss students' writing with them

Activity #1
    Choose one of the review games/activities included in the packet and spend your class period as outlined there. Some materials for these activities are located in the Extra Activities Packet section of this unit.

Activity #2
    Remind students that the Unit Test will be in the next class meeting. Stress the review of the Study Guides and their class notes as a last minute, brush-up review for homework.

Activity #3
    While the class is involved with the review exercise(s), call individual students to your desk or some other private area to hold writing conferences. Writing assignments 1 and 2 should be completed and graded by this time; they should be the basis of your conferences. An evaluation form is included with this unit for your convenience.

WRITING ASSIGNMENT #3 - *A Tale of Two Cities*

PROMPT
You have spent some time looking at the cities of Paris and London. This assignment comes closer to home: persuade your pen-pal from either London or Paris that he/she should come to your town to live -- OR -- persuade a friend of yours who lives in your town to go with you to Paris or London to live.

PREWRITING
Divide a sheet of notebook paper into thirds by drawing two vertical lines down the page. In the left-hand column, make a list of the qualities that make a place a good place to live. In the middle column make notes about how well you town fulfills each quality you have written in the left-hand column. In the right column, make notes about how well either Paris or London fulfills each quality. Analyze the information on your chart to determine whether, in your opinion, your town is the better place to live.

DRAFTING
Use a friendly letter format. In your first paragraph introduce the idea that you want your pen pal to move to your town OR that you want your friend to move with you to Paris or London.

In the body of your letter you should write one paragraph for each of the qualities you wrote down in your prewriting chart. Within each paragraph, explain why or how your town OR Paris or London fulfills the quality about which the paragraph is written.

In your concluding paragraph, summarize the reasons why your pen pal should move to your town OR why your friend should move with you to Paris or London.

PROMPT
When you finish the rough draft of your paper, ask a student who sits near you to read it. After reading your rough draft, he/she should tell you what he/she liked best about your work, which parts were difficult to understand, and ways in which your work could be improved. Reread your paper considering your critic's comments, and make the corrections you think are necessary.

PROOFREADING
Do a final proofreading of your paper double-checking your grammar, spelling, organization, and the clarity of your ideas.

WRITING EVALUATION FORM - *A Tale of Two Cities*

Name _____ Date _____

Grade _____

Circle One For Each Item:

Grammar:	correct errors noted on paper
Spelling:	correct errors noted on paper
Punctuation:	correct errors noted on paper
Legibility:	excellent good fair poor
_____	excellent good fair poor
_____	excellent good fair poor

Strengths:

Weaknesses:

Comments/Suggestions:

REVIEW GAMES/ACTIVITIES - *A Tale of Two Cities*

1. Ask the class to make up a unit test for *A Tale of Two Cities*. The test should have 4 sections: matching, true/false, short answer, and essay. Students may use 1/2 period to make the test and then swap papers and use the other 1/2 class period to take a test a classmate has devised. (open book) You may want to use the unit test included in this packet or take questions from the students' unit tests to formulate your own test.

2. Take 1/2 period for students to make up true and false questions (including the answers). Collect the papers and divide the class into two teams. Draw a big tic-tac-toe board on the chalk board. Make one team X and one team O. Ask questions to each side, giving each student one turn. If the question is answered correctly, that students' team's letter (X or O) is placed in the box. If the answer is incorrect, no mark is placed in the box. The object is to get three marks in a row like tic-tac-toe. You may want to keep track of the number of games won for each team.

3. Take 1/2 period for students to make up questions (true/false and short answer). Collect the questions. Divide the class into two teams. You'll alternate asking questions to individual members of teams A & B (like in a spelling bee). The question keeps going from A to B until it is correctly answered, then a new question is asked. A correct answer does not allow the team to get another question. Correct answers are +2 points; incorrect answers are -1 point.

4. Have students pair up and quiz each other from their study guides and class notes.

5. Give students *A Tale of Two Cities* crossword puzzle to complete.

6. Divide your class into two teams. Use the *A Tale of Two Cities* crossword words with their letters jumbled as a word list. Student 1 from Team A faces off against Student 1 from Team B. You write the first jumbled word on the board. The first student (1A or 1B) to unscramble the word wins the chance for his/her team to score points. If 1A wins the jumble, go to student 2A and give him/her a clue. He/she must give you the correct word which matches that clue. If he/she does, Team A scores a point, and you give student 3A a clue for which you expect another correct response. Continue giving Team A clues until some team member makes an incorrect response. An incorrect response sends the game back to the jumbled-word face off, this time with students 2A and 2B. Instead of repeating giving clues to the first few students of each team, continue with the student after the one who gave the last incorrect response on the team. For example, if Team B wins the jumbled-word face-off, and student 5B gave the last incorrect answer for Team B, you would start this round of clue questions with student 6B, and so on. The team with the most points wins!

UNIT TESTS

SHORT ANSWER UNIT TEST 1 - *A Tale of Two Cities*

I. Matching/Identify

___ Lorry	A. Lucie's friend/servant
___ Lucie	B. Jerry was a messenger there
___ Dr. Manette	C. Spy; supposed to be dead
___ Pross	D. "Let them eat grass."
___ Ernest Defarge	E. Renounces his family's name
___ Jacques	F. Takes Lucie to her father
___ Jerry Cruncher	G. Darnay's uncle
___ Charles Darnay	H. A prison
___ Sydney Carton	I. Solomon Pross
___ Stryver	J. Part-time grave-robber
___ Cly	K. Takes Darnay's place at the guillotine
___ Barsad	L. Marries Charles
___ Marquis St. Evermonde	M. Keeps the register
___ Gabelle	N. Asked Charles to come to France
___ Foulon	O. Cobbling
___ The Vengeance	P. Madame Defarge's lieutenant
___ Madame Defarge	Q. Wine shop keeper
___ Bastille	R. Any revolutionary
___ Tellsons	S. Carton's employer; attorney

A Tale of Two Cities Short Answer Unit Test 1 Page Two
II. Short Answer
1. Dickens uses the broken cask of wine's spilling in the street to foreshadow what future event?

2. Why did someone stab the Marquis (and kill him)?

3. What promise did Sydney Carton make to Lucie?

4. Why did Charles Darnay go to France?

5. Why was Dr. Manette popular in Paris?

6. Why was Charles arrested again on the day of his release?

A Tale of Two Cities Short Answer Unit Test 1 Page Three

7. What does Carton get from Barsad?

8. Why was Charles sentenced to death?

9. How was Madame Defarge "cheated"?

10. How did Carton "redeem" himself?

III. Composition
      What is the point of *A Tale of Two Cities*? When we read books, we usually come away from our reading experience a little richer, having given more thought of a particular aspect of life. What do you think Charles Dickens intended us to gain from reading his novel?

A Tale of Two Cities Short Answer Unit Test 1 Page Four

IV. Vocabulary
	Listen to the vocabulary words and write them down. Go back later and fill in the correct definition for each word.
1.

2.

3.

4.

5.

6.

7.

8.

9.

10.

KEY: SHORT ANSWER UNIT TEST #1 - *A Tale of Two Cities*

I. Matching

_F_ Lorry		A. Lucie's friend/servant
_L_ Lucie		B. Jerry was a messenger there
_O_ Dr. Manette		C. Spy; supposed to be dead
_A_ Pross		D. "Let them eat grass."
_Q_ Ernest Defarge		E. Renounces his family's name
_R_ Jacques		F. Takes Lucie to her father
_J_ Jerry Cruncher		G. Darnay's uncle
_E_ Charles Darnay		H. A prison
_K_ Sydney Carton		I. Solomon Pross
_S_ Stryver		J. Part-time grave-robber
_C_ Cly		K. Takes Darnay's place at the guillotine
_I_ Barsad		L. Marries Charles
_G_ Marquis St. Evremonde		M. Keeps the register
_N_ Gabelle		N. Asked Charles to come to France
_D_ Foulon		O. Cobbling
_P_ The Vengeance		P. Madame Defarge's lieutenant
_M_ Madame Defarge		Q. Wine shop keeper
_H_ Bastille		R. Any revolutionary
_B_ Tellsons		S. Carton's employer; attorney

II. Short Answer

1. Dickens uses the broken cask of wine's spilling in the street to foreshadow what future event?
    The time will come when blood will be spilled in the streets and people will be stained with it as they are stained with the spilled wine.

2. Why did someone stab the Marquis (and kill him)?
    He was killed because of his careless and inhumane attitude when his carriage ran over a child.

3. What promise did Sydney Carton make to Lucie?
    He promised her that he would sacrifice himself for those she loves.

4. Why did Charles Darnay go to France?
    His family's loyal servant, Gabelle, had been imprisoned, and Charles went to try to help him out.

5. Why was Dr. Manette popular in Paris?
    He had been a prisoner at the Bastille, a victim of the aristocracy.

6. Why was Charles arrested again on the day of his release?
    He had been denounced by the Defarges and another person (we later find out was Dr. Manette in his letter).

7. What does Carton get from Barsad?
    He gets Barsad to promise him entry to see Charles Darnay one time before Darnay's execution, should that arise.

8. Why was Charles sentenced to death?
    He was sentenced to death to atone for the sins of his family against the common people.

9. How was Madame Defarge "cheated"?
    Darnay escaped execution and her hopes of total "extermination" of the aristocracy were never realized.

10. How did Carton "redeem" himself?
    He switched places with Darnay in the cell and went to the guillotine for him for Lucie's sake.

III. Composition
    Grade on your own criteria.

IV. Vocabulary

Choose ten of the following vocabulary words. Read them orally to your class to the students can write them down on part IV of their vocabulary tests.

ABATE	To lessen
ACQUIESCENCE	Compliance
ALACRITY	Liveliness; cheerful readiness
ANATOMISE	Dissect; analyze
ANTIPATHY	Dislike; opposition
APPROBATION	Approval; liking
ASSENTED	Agreed
ASSIDUOUSLY	Constantly; diligently
ATHEISTICAL	Not believing in God
AVOCATIONS	Occupations
CAPRICIOUS	Whimsical
DEBAUCHERY	Habitual bad conduct
DISCERNIBLE	Distinguishable
DISSONANCE	Discord; disagreement in sound
DUBIOUSLY	Uncertain; doubtful
ENGENDERED	To be caused or produced
FERVENT	Earnest
GESTICULATION	Making motions (usually with hands) while speaking
IMPERIOUS	Haughty; arrogant; domineering
IMPERTURBABLE	Unmovable; calm; can't be bothered
INCORRIGIBLE	Bad beyond correction or reform
INEXORABLE	Unbending; unrelenting
LENIENT	Having an indulgent, mild disposition
MANIFEST	Evident; obvious
OBLIVION	State of being forgotten
OSTENTATIOUS	Ambitious display; great showing of something
PORTENTOUSLY	Ominously; foreshadowing something bad
PRODIGIOUS	Extraordinary; huge
PROPITIATE	Atone; make amends
REDUNDANCY	Using or having more than necessary
RETINUE	A train of attendants
SAGACITY	Shrewdness; intelligence
SPECTRAL	Ghostly
STEEPED	Soaked
SUPPLICATION	Humble begging
UNFATHOMABLE	Incomprehensible; beyond belief
VOCIFERATING	Crying out loudly

SHORT ANSWER UNIT TEST 2 - *A Tale of Two Cities*

I. Matching

___ Lorry   A. Renounces his family's name

___ Lucie   B. Solomon Pross

___ Dr. Manette   C. Part-time grave-robber

___ Pross   D. Takes Darnay's place at the guillotine

___ Ernest Defarge   E. Marries Charles

___ Jacques   F. Madame Defarge's lieutenant

___ Jerry Cruncher   G. Darnay's uncle

___ Charles Darnay   H. Cobbling

___ Sydney Carton   I. Asked Charles to come to France

___ Stryver   J. Wine shop keeper

___ Cly   K. "Let them eat grass."

___ Barsad   L. Any revolutionary

___ Marquis St. Evremonde   M. Takes Lucie to her father

___ Gabelle   N. Carton's employer; attorney

___ Foulon   O. A prison

___ The Vengeance   P. Keeps the register

___ Madame Defarge   Q. Spy; supposed to be dead

___ Bastille   R. Lucie's friend/servant

___ Tellsons   S. Jerry was a messenger there

A Tale of Two Cities Short Answer Unit Test 2 Page 2

II. Short Answer

1. Dickens describes England and France in 1775. How does he compare them? (1)

2. Explain the meaning of "recalled to life." (4)

3. Dickens uses the broken cask of wine's spilling in the street to foreshadow what future event? (5)

4. Charles visits his uncle the Marquis and informs him that he renounces his name and property. Why does Charles Darnay do this? (9)

5. Why is it foolish of Charles Darnay to go to France? (24)

6. Why does the crowd at the grindstone take up Dr. Manette's cause to free Charles? (2)

7. Sydney Carton said he would die young because of a dissipated and wasted life. How was he both right and wrong? (15)

8. How is Madame Defarge cheated? (15)

A Tale of Two Cities Short Answer Unit Test 2 Page 3

III. Composition
    Write a paragraph answering each of the following:

1. Where is the climax of the story? Defend your choice.

2. What are the main conflicts in the story and how are they resolved?

3. Explain the use and importance of knitting and cobbling.

4. Compare and contrast Stryver and Carton.

A Tale of Two Cities Short Answer Unit Test 2 Page 4

IV. Vocabulary
 Listen to the vocabulary words and write them down. Go back later and fill in the correct definition for each word.

1.

2.

3.

4.

5.

6.

7.

8.

9.

10.

KEY: SHORT ANSWER UNIT TEST 2 *A Tale of Two Cities*

I. Matching (Use this matching key also for the Advanced Short Answer Unit Test)

M	1. Lorry		A. Renounces his family's name
E	2. Lucie		B. Solomon Pross
H	3. Dr. Manette		C. Part-time grave-robber
R	4. Pross		D. Takes Darnay's place at the guillotine
J	5. Ernest Defarge		E. Marries Charles
L	6. Jacques		F. Madame Defarge's lieutenant
C	7. Jerry Cruncher		G. Darnay's uncle
A	8. Charles Darnay		H. Cobbling
D	9. Sydney Carton		I. Asked Charles to come to France
N	10. Stryver		J. Wine shop keeper
Q	11. Cly		K. "Let them eat grass."
B	12. Barsad		L. Any revolutionary
G	13. Marquis St. Evremonde		M. Takes Lucie to her father
I	14. Gabelle		N. Carton's employer; attorney
K	15. Foulon		O. A prison
F	16. The Vengeance		P. Keeps the register
P	17. Madame Defarge		Q. Spy; supposed to be dead
O	18. Bastille		R. Lucie's friend/servant
S	19. Tellsons		S. Jerry was a messenger there

II. Short Answer

1. Dickens describes England and France in 1775. How does he compare them? (1)
    Both are ruled by kings who enjoy divine right and appear to believe the status quo is not only unimpeachable but everlasting as well.

2. Explain the meaning of "recalled to life." (4)
    A man has been released after 18 years in prison in France.

3. Dickens uses the broken cask of wine's spilling in the street to foreshadow what future event?
    The time will come when blood will be spilled in the streets and people will be stained with it as they are stained with the spilled wine.

4. Charles visits his uncle the Marquis and informs him that he renounces his name and property. Why does Charles Darnay do this? (9)
    His mother's dying wish was that Charles would redress the family's many wrongs and cruelties, and that he would lighten the burden of his subjects in the village.

5. Why is it foolish of Charles Darnay to go to France? (24)
    He is a member of the nobility, and even though he has renounced his title, he puts himself in grave danger by returning to France at this time.

6. Why does the crowd at the grindstone take up Dr. Manette's cause to free Charles? (2)
    Because he was once a prisoner at the Bastille, Dr. Manette is a sort of a folk hero. Anyone imprisoned by the old regime is automatically supported and admired.

7. Sydney Carton said he would die young because of a dissipated and wasted life. How was he both right and wrong? (15)
    He does die young, but for reasons of love and sacrifice. His death gives him the honor he never attained in life.

8. How is Madame Defarge cheated? (15)
    The one man she wished to see die, more than all others, lives, although without her knowledge, and she cannot reach his wife or child. Her wish for total extermination is not going to come true.

III. Composition
    Grade on your own criteria.

IV. Vocabulary
    See Key: Short Answer Unit Test 1, Part IV for a list of words and directions.

ADVANCED SHORT ANSWER UNIT TEST - *A Tale of Two Cities*

I. Matching

___ Lorry				A. Renounces his family's name

___ Lucie				B. Solomon Pross

___ Dr. Manette			C. Part-time grave-robber

___ Pross				D. Takes Darnay's place at the guillotine

___ Ernest Defarge		E. Marries Charles

___ Jacques			F. Madame Defarge's lieutenant

___ Jerry Cruncher		G. Darnay's uncle

___ Charles Darnay		H. Cobbling

___ Sydney Carton		I. Asked Charles to come to France

___ Stryver			J. Wine shop keeper

___ Cly				K. "Let them eat grass."

___ Barsad			L. Any revolutionary

___ Marquis St. Evremonde	M. Takes Lucie to her father

___ Gabelle			N. Carton's employer; attorney

___ Foulon			O. A prison

___ The Vengeance		P. Keeps the register

___ Madame Defarge		Q. Spy; supposed to be dead

___ Bastille			R. Lucie's friend/servant

___ Tellsons			S. Jerry was a messenger there

A Tale of Two Cities Advanced Short Answer Unit Test Page 2

II. Composition   Answer each of the following with a complete paragraph:

1. Characterize Charles Dickens's style and explain how it affects our perception of his work.

2. Explain how in *A Tale of Two Cities* "future" generations are affected by the past.

3. Explain the use and importance of knitting and cobbling.

4. Explain the roles of these characters in the story: Barsad, Cruncher, Gabelle, Mr. Lorry, Marquis de St. Evremonde, and Stryver. How was each of these characters important?

5. Compare and contrast Stryver and Carton.

A Tale of Two Cities Advanced Short Answer Unit Test Page 3

6. Discuss Dickens's use of symbolism in *A Tale of Two Cities*.

7. What are the main themes/ideas presented in *A Tale of Two Cities*?

8. In what way(s) is *A Tale of Two Cities* a story about good versus evil?

9. Compare and contrast London and Paris (relating to *A Tale of Two Cities*).

10. Explain the use of the theme or conflict of death versus life in *A Tale of Two Cities*.

A Tale of Two Cities Advanced Short Answer Unit Test Page 4

III. Essay

"It was the best of times, it was the worst of times, it was the age of wisdom, it was the age of foolishness, it was the epoch of belief, it was the epoch of incredulity, it was the season of Light, it was the season of Darkness, it was the spring of hope, it was the winter of despair, we had everything before us, we had nothing before us, we were all going direct to Heaven, we were all going direct the other way--. . . . "

Explain how this first paragraph of the book perfectly sets the stage for the rest of the novel.

A Tale of Two Cities Advanced Short Answer Unit Test Page 5

IV. Vocabulary

Listen to the vocabulary words and write them down. Go back later and write a composition in which you use all of the words. The composition must relate in some way to *A Tale of Two Cities*.

MULTIPLE CHOICE UNIT TEST 1 - *A Tale of Two Cities*

I. Matching

___ 1. Lorry   A. Lucie's friend/servant

___ 2. Lucie   B. Jerry was a messenger there

___ 3. Dr. Manette   C. Spy; supposed to be dead

___ 4. Pross   D. "Let them eat grass."

___ 5. Ernest Defarge   E. Renounces his family's name

___ 6. Jacques   F. Takes Lucie to her father

___ 7. Jerry Cruncher   G. Darnay's uncle

___ 8. Charles Darnay   H. A prison

___ 9. Sydney Carton   I. Solomon Pross

___ 10. Stryver   J. Part-time grave-robber

___ 11. Cly   K. Takes Darnay's place at the guillotine

___ 12. Barsad   L. Marries Charles

___ 13. Marquis St. Evremonde   M. Keeps the register

___ 14. Gabelle   N. Asked Charles to come to France

___ 15. Foulon   O. Cobbling

___ 16. The Vengeance   P. Madame Defarge's lieutenant

___ 17. Madame Defarge   Q. Wine shop keeper

___ 18. Bastille   R. Any revolutionary

___ 19. Tellsons   S. Carton's employer; attorney

A Tale of Two Cities Multiple Choice Unit Test 1 Page 2
II. Multiple Choice
1. Dickens describes England and France in 1775. How does he compare them?
  a. Both are engaged in wars with their colonies.
  b. Both are ruled by kings who enjoy divine right and appear to believe the status quo is unimpeachable and everlasting.
  c. Both are ruled by royal families who are at the end of their lines.
  d. Both governments are on the brink of collapse.

2. How does Dickens describe human beings?
  a. We all have good in us; no one is all bad.
  b. We are an unreliable and greedy bunch.
  c. We are a secret and a mystery to each other.
  d. We are a despicable, wretched race.

3. Explain the meaning of "recalled to life."
  a. A man has been released after 18 years in prison.
  b. A man was revived after being thought dead.
  c. A retired spy was put back into service.
  d. A man who had given up on life met a woman who once again gave him the will to live.

4. Dickens uses the broken cask of wine's spilling in the street to foreshadow what future event?
  a. The death of Dr. Manette
  b. The American Revolution
  c. The French Revolution
  d. The death of the kings

5. What is the significance of so many "Jacques" in Defarge's wine shop?
  a. It is just a common name in France--like "Bill" is in America.
  b. It is a common name for a butler, who would be sent to get wine for the family.
  c. It is the common name for "customer" or "friend."
  d. It is a common name for members of the revolution.

6. How does Dickens describe the privileged class in France?
  a. Concerned do-gooders
  b. Conservative, intelligent, kind
  c. Self-centered but intelligent and benevolent
  d. Extravagant, superficial and useless

A Tale of Two Cities Multiple Choice Unit Test 1 Page 3

7. Charles visits his uncle the Marquis and informs him that he renounces his name and property. Why does Charles Darnay do this?
    a. Because he felt guilty
    b. To honor his mother's dying wish
    c. To impress Lucie
    d. To help the revolution

8. In the conversation between the Marquis and Charles, Dickens gives a hint that at one time the Marquis was able to have someone imprisoned. Who?
    a. Charles
    b. Dr. Manette
    c. Lucie
    d. Stryver

9. Why was the Marquis killed?
    a. It was an accident; the mob crushed him
    b. His carriage overturned.
    c. The aristocrats found out he had been helping the common people and the revolution.
    d. The common people rose up against him for running down the child and his careless attitude about the incident.

10. Why doesn't Dr. Manette want Charles to reveal his true name?
    a. He suspects a connection between his past imprisonment and Charles's family.
    b. It would upset Lucie.
    c. He thinks Madame Defarge might find out his true identity.
    d. He doesn't trust Charles.

11. What promise does Sydney Carton make to Lucie?
    a. He will destroy Stryver for her.
    b. He will take care of her father.
    c. He would sacrifice himself for those she loves.
    d. He would gladly marry her to help her "save face" in her broken engagement to Stryver.

12. What "fish" does Cruncher go fishing after?
    a. Revolutionaries
    b. Madame Defarge's list of names
    c. Aristocrats
    d. Dead bodies

A Tale of Two Cities Multiple Choice Unit Test 1 Page 4

13. Why does Madame Defarge wear a rose in her hair?
    a. She is an ugly woman trying to look pretty.
    b. The rose is a signal that a spy is in the shop.
    c. She hides secret messages in it for revolutionaries to pick up when they greet her with a hug.
    d. The rose isn't functional. It is Dickens' symbol for the blossoming revolution. The scarlet color is the color of blood shed in the revolution.

14. Lucie's fanciful thought years ago of the echoes of a multitude of footsteps becomes a reality in France. What has occurred?
    a. The mob has destroyed Paris.
    b. The mob has destroyed innocent victims.
    c. The mob has stormed the Bastille in Paris.
    d. The mob has stormed the countryside.

15. Why is it foolish of Charles Darnay to go to France?
    a. Dr. Manette and Lucie need him at home.
    b. Madame Defarge has put out a contract on him.
    c. He is a member of the French nobility.
    d. He has no money, no connections, and no chance to help Mr. Lorry anyway.

16. Why does the crowd at the grindstone take up Dr. Manette's cause to free Charles?
    a. Madame Defarge has spread the word that Darnay must be freed.
    b. Dr. Manette is a persuasive speaker and leader. The mob would have followed anyone in their frenzy.
    c. Dr. Manette is a folk hero, so the people support his cause.
    d. This is just another good example of Dickens' use of coincidence.

17. What caused the jury to acquit Charles?
    a. He renounced his title.
    b. He came to the aid of Gabelle.
    c. He had been tried in England for treason.
    d. All of the above

18. Why is Charles condemned to die?
    a. He killed Madame Defarge's older sister.
    b. He has committed treason.
    c. He must pay for the evils of his family, especially his father and uncle.
    d. His death is just for the new regime to show its power. He is an unlucky victim.

A Tale of Two Cities Multiple Choice Unit Test 1 Page 5

19. Sydney Carton said he would die young because of _____.
    a. A dissipated and wasted life
    b. Love and sacrifice
    c. Hatred and greed
    d. Accidental suicide

20. How is Madame Defarge cheated?
    a. She never holds an office in the new government.
    b. The register is robbed.
    c. Her wish of total extermination will never come true.
    d. Lucie and Miss Pross escape.

A Tale of Two Cities Multiple Choice Unit Test 1 Page 6

III. Composition

      Who is the central character in *A Tale of Two Cities*? Defend your choice by showing how this character relates to the themes and conflicts in the story.

A Tale of Two Cities Multiple Choice Unit Test 1 Page 7

IV. Vocabulary
   Match the correct definitions to the words.

___ 1. Sagacity   a. Evident; obvious

___ 2. Approbation   b. Haughty; arrogant; domineering

___ 3. Steeped   c. Approval; liking

___ 4. Retinue   d. To lessen

___ 5. Avocations   e. Dislike; opposition

___ 6. Oblivion   f. Habitual bad conduct

___ 7. Incorrigible   g. Humble begging

___ 8. Supplication   h. State of being forgotten

___ 9. Fervent   i. Earnest

___ 10. Abate   j. Ominously; foreshadowing something bad

___ 11. Anatomise   k. Agreed

___ 12. Spectral   l. Ghostly

___ 13. Manifest   m. Not believing in god

___ 14. Antipathy   n. Compliance

___ 15. Assented   o. Shrewdness; intelligence

___ 16. Debauchery   p. Occupations

___ 17. Atheistical   q. Bad beyond correction or reform

___ 18. Imperious   r. A train of attendants

___ 19. Portentously   s. Dissect; analyze

___ 20. Acquiescence   t. Soaked

MULTIPLE CHOICE UNIT TEST 2 - *A Tale of Two Cities*

I. Matching

___ 1. Lorry   A. Renounces his family's name

___ 2. Lucie   B. Solomon Pross

___ 3. Dr. Manette   C. Part-time grave-robber

___ 4. Pross   D. Takes Darnay's place at the guillotine

___ 5. Ernest Defarge   E. Marries Charles

___ 6. Jacques   F. Madame Defarge's lieutenant

___ 7. Jerry Cruncher   G. Darnay's uncle

___ 8. Charles Darnay   H. Cobbling

___ 9. Sydney Carton   I. Asked Charles to come to France

___ 10. Stryver   J. Wine shop keeper

___ 11. Cly   K. "Let them eat grass."

___ 12. Barsad   L. Any revolutionary

___ 13. Marquis St. Evremonde   M. Takes Lucie to her father

___ 14. Gabelle   N. Carton's employer; attorney

___ 15. Foulon   O. A prison

___ 16. The Vengeance   P. Keeps the register

___ 17. Madame Defarge   Q. Spy; supposed to be dead

___ 18. Bastille   R. Lucie's friend/servant

___ 19. Tellsons   S. Jerry was a messenger there

A Tale of Two Cities Multiple Choice Unit Test 2 Page 2

II. Multiple Choice

1. Dickens describes England and France in 1775. How does he compare them?
    a. Both are engaged in wars with their colonies.
    b. Both governments are on the brink of collapse.
    c. Both are ruled by royal families who are at the end of their lines.
    d. Both are ruled by kings who enjoy divine right and appear to believe the status quo is unimpeachable and everlasting.

2. How does Dickens describe human beings?
    a. We are a secret and a mystery to each other.
    b. We are an unreliable and greedy bunch.
    c. We all have good in us; no one is all bad.
    d. We are a despicable, wretched race.

3. Explain the meaning of "recalled to life."
    a. A man was revived after being thought dead.
    b. A man has been released after 18 years in prison.
    c. A retired spy was put back into service.
    d. A man who had given up on life met a woman who once again gave him the will to live.

4. Dickens uses the broken cask of wine's spilling in the street to foreshadow what future event?
    a. The death of Dr. Manette
    b. The American Revolution
    c. The death of the kings
    d. The French Revolution

5. What is the significance of so many "Jacques" in Defarge's wine shop?
    a. It is just a common name in France--like "Bill" is in America.
    b. It is a common name for a butler, who would be sent to get wine for the family.
    c. It is a common name for members of the revolution.
    d. It is the common name for "customer" or "friend."

6. How does Dickens describe the privileged class in France?
    a. Concerned do-gooders
    b. Extravagant, superficial and useless
    c. Self-centered but intelligent and benevolent
    d. Conservative, intelligent, kind

A Tale of Two Cities Multiple Choice Unit Test 2 Page 3

7. Charles visits his uncle the Marquis and informs him that he renounces his name and property. Why does Charles Darnay do this?
    a. Because he felt guilty
    b. To help the revolution
    c. To impress Lucie
    d. To honor his mother's dying wish

8. In the conversation between the Marquis and Charles, Dickens gives a hint that at one time the Marquis was able to have someone imprisoned. Who?
    a. Dr. Manette
    b. Charles
    c. Lucie
    d. Stryver

9. Why was the Marquis killed?
    a. The common people rose up against him for running down the child and his careless attitude about the incident.
    b. His carriage overturned.
    c. The aristocrats found out he had been helping the common people and the revolution.
    d. It was an accident; the mob crushed him

10. Why doesn't Dr. Manette want Charles to reveal his true name?
    a. It would upset Lucie.
    b. He suspects a connection between his past imprisonment and Charles's family.
    c. He thinks Madame Defarge might find out his true identity.
    d. He doesn't trust Charles.

11. What promise does Sydney Carton make to Lucie?
    a. He will destroy Stryver for her.
    b. He will take care of her father.
    c. He would gladly marry her to help her "save face" in her broken engagement to Stryver.
    d. He would sacrifice himself for those she loves.

12. What "fish" does Cruncher go fishing after?
    a. Revolutionaries
    b. Madame Defarge's list of names
    c. Dead bodies
    d. Aristocrats

A Tale of Two Cities Multiple Choice Unit Test 2 Page 4

13. Why does Madame Defarge wear a rose in her hair?
    a. She is an ugly woman trying to look pretty.
    b. The rose isn't functional. It is Dickens' symbol for the blossoming revolution. The scarlet color is the color of blood shed in the revolution.
    c. She hides secret messages in it for revolutionaries to pick up when they greet her with a hug.
    d. The rose is a signal that a spy is in the shop.

14. Lucie's fanciful thought years ago of the echoes of a multitude of footsteps becomes a reality in France. What has occurred?
    a. The mob has stormed the Bastille in Paris.
    b. The mob has destroyed innocent victims.
    c. The mob has destroyed Paris.
    d. The mob has stormed the countryside.

15. Why is it foolish of Charles Darnay to go to France?
    a. Dr. Manette and Lucie need him at home.
    b. He is a member of the French nobility.
    c. Madame Defarge has put out a contract on him.
    d. He has no money, no connections, and no chance to help Mr. Lorry anyway.

16. Why does the crowd at the grindstone take up Dr. Manette's cause to free Charles?
    a. Madame Defarge has spread the word that Darnay must be freed.
    b. Dr. Manette is a persuasive speaker and leader. The mob would have followed anyone in their frenzy.
    c. This is just another good example of Dickens' use of coincidence.
    d. Dr. Manette is a folk hero, so the people support his cause.

17. What caused the jury to acquit Charles?
    a. He renounced his title.
    b. He came to the aid of Gabelle.
    c. He had been tried in England for treason.
    d. All of the above

18. Why is Charles condemned to die?
    a. He must pay for the evils of his family, especially his father and uncle.
    b. He has committed treason.
    c. He killed Madame Defarge's older sister.
    d. His death is just for the new regime to show its power. He is an unlucky victim.

A Tale of Two Cities Multiple Choice Unit Test 2 Page 5

19. Sydney Carton said he would die young because of _____.
    a. Hatred and greed
    b. Love and sacrifice
    c. A dissipated and wasted life
    d. Accidental suicide

20. How is Madame Defarge cheated?
    a. She never holds an office in the new government.
    b. Her wish of total extermination will never come true.
    c. The register is robbed.
    d. Lucie and Miss Pross escape.

A Tale of Two Cities Multiple Choice Unit Test 2 Page 6

III. Composition
　　Choose one adjective to describe each of the following characters. After making your choice, write a paragraph for each in which you explain why your adjective is appropriate.

Madame Defarge

Stryver

Charles Darnay

Lucie

Dr. Manette

Marquis St. Evremonde

Lorry

A Tale of Two Cities Multiple Choice Unit Test 2 Page 7

IV. Vocabulary   Match the correct definitions to the words.

___ 1. Steeped   a. Haughty; arrogant; domineering

___ 2. Propitiate   b. Agreed

___ 3. Dissonance   c. Constantly; diligently

___ 4. Prodigious   d. Dissect; analyze

___ 5. Incorrigible   e. Habitual bad conduct

___ 6. Dubiously   f. To lessen

___ 7. Debauchery   g. Bad beyond correction or reform

___ 8. Anatomise   h. Approval; liking

___ 9. Assiduously   i. Liveliness; cheerful readiness

___ 10. Sagacity   j. Shrewdness; intelligence

___ 11. Oblivion   k. Extraordinary; huge

___ 12. Vociferating   l. Evident; obvious

___ 13. Alacrity   m. Ominously; foreshadowing something bad

___ 14. Supplication   n. Uncertain; doubtful

___ 15. Portentously   o. Soaked

___ 16. Imperious   p. Atone; make amends

___ 17. Manifest   q. Discord; disagreement in sound

___ 18. Abate   r. State of being forgotten

___ 19. Approbation   s. Humble begging

___ 20. Assented   t. Crying out loudly

ANSWER SHEET - *A Tale of Two Cities*
Multiple Choice Unit Tests

I. Matching
1. ___
2. ___
3. ___
4. ___
5. ___
6. ___
7. ___
8. ___
9. ___
10. ___
11. ___
12. ___
13. ___
14. ___
15. ___
16. ___
17. ___
18. ___
19. ___

II. Multiple Choice
1. ___
2. ___
3. ___
4. ___
5. ___
6. ___
7. ___
8. ___
9. ___
10. ___
11. ___
12. ___
13. ___
14. ___
15. ___
16. ___
17. ___
18. ___
19. ___
20. ___

IV. Vocabulary
1. ___
2. ___
3. ___
4. ___
5. ___
6. ___
7. ___
8. ___
9. ___
10. ___
11. ___
12. ___
13. ___
14. ___
15. ___
16. ___
17. ___
18. ___
19. ___
20. ___

ANSWER KEY - *A Tale of Two Cities*
Multiple Choice Unit Tests

Answers to Unit Test 1 are in the left column. Answers to Unit Test 2 are in the right column.

I. Matching	II. Multiple Choice	IV. Vocabulary
1. F M	1. B D	1. O O
2. L E	2. D D	2. C P
3. O H	3. A B	3. T Q
4. A R	4. C D	4. R K
5. Q J	5. D C	5. P G
6. R L	6. D B	6. H N
7. J C	7. B D	7. Q E
8. E A	8. B A	8. G D
9. K D	9. D A	9. I C
10. S N	10. A B	10. D J
11. C Q	11. C D	11. S R
12. I B	12. D C	12. L T
13. G G	13. B D	13. A I
14. N I	14. C A	14. E S
15. D K	15. C B	15. K M
16. P F	16. C D	16. F A
17. M P	17. D D	17. M L
18. H O	18. C A	18. B F
19. B S	19. A C	19. J H
	20. B B	20. N B

UNIT RESOURCE MATERIALS

BULLETIN BOARD IDEAS - *A Tale of Two Cities*

1. Save one corner of the board for the best of students' A Tale Of Two Cities writing assignments.

2. Take one of the word search puzzles from the extra activities packet and with a marker copy it over in a large size on the bulletin board. Write the clue words to find to one side. Invite students prior to and after class to find the words and circle them on the bulletin board. Cut out letters to title the board, "A SEARCH FOR TWO CITIES."

3. Title the board A Tale Of Two Cities: A NOVEL FULL OF CHARACTERS. Find pictures in magazines (or perhaps your library has a file of pictures) of people who look like the various characters in the novel. Place the pictures on colorful paper, write the character's name under the picture (or next to it) and write a brief description of the character by it.

4. Title the board A TALE OF TWO CITIES. On colorful paper post pictures of things people would see while touring Paris and France. Your local travel agency could probably help you find some nice pictures or brochures.

5. Title the board CHARLES DICKENS (1812 - 1870). In the center of the board, post an article summarizing his life. Around that, staple up book jackets or cut-out "books" (from construction paper) with the titles of his most famous works showing. You may wish to write names of some of his most memorable characters from these works near the appropriate "book."

6. Do a bulletin board about the French Revolution, giving brief explanation of the cause and result of the revolution. You could use a map of France as a graphic aide, and perhaps your local library would have some other pictures you could borrow. Check with your school's history department to see if they have any pictures.

7. Title the board: A TALE OF TWO CITIES. Put up a map of Europe. Highlight France and England. Mark Paris and London with big red stars.

EXTRA ACTIVITIES

One of the difficulties in teaching a novel is that all students don't read at the same speed. One student who likes to read may take the book home and finish it in a day or two. Sometimes a few students finish the in-class assignments early. The problem, then, is finding suitable extra activities for students.

One thing that helps is to keep a little library in the classroom. For this unit on A Tale of Two Cities, you might check out from the school library other related books and articles about the French Revolution, France, Paris, England, London, or history of the period. Other works by or biographical information about Charles Dickens might interest some students. Also, information about careers as a wine shop keeper, lawyer, banker or shoe-making industry might be helpful for some students.

Other things you may keep on hand are puzzles. We have made some relating directly to *A Tale of Two Cities* for you. Feel free to duplicate them.

Some students may like to draw. You might devise a contest or allow some extra-credit grade for students who draw characters or scenes from *A Tale of Two Cities*. Note, too, that if the students do not want to keep their drawings you may pick up some extra bulletin board materials this way. If you have a contest and you supply the prize (a record album or something like that perhaps), you could, possibly, make the drawing itself a non-refundable entry fee.

The pages which follow contain games, puzzles and worksheets. The keys, when appropriate, immediately follow the puzzle or worksheet. There are two main groups of activities: one group for the unit; that is, generally relating to the *A Tale of Two Cities* text, and another group of activities related strictly to the *A Tale of Two Cities* vocabulary.

Directions for these games, puzzles and worksheets are self-explanatory. The object here is to provide you with extra materials you may use in any way you choose.

MORE ACTIVITIES - *A Tale of Two Cities*

1. Pick a chapter or scene with a great deal of dialogue and have the students act it out on a stage. (Perhaps you could assign various scenes to different groups of students so more than one scene could be acted and more students could participate.)

2. Have students make a model maps of Paris or London.

3. Have students make "A Tale of _____" (Fill in your town's name.) Assign each student a different aspects of your town to gather information about: history, population, government, educational opportunities, services provided, economic base, jobs available, etc. Have all students bring in their information and do a group writing assignment to compile the information into a booklet. Print it up and give copies to the libraries and newspapers in your area.

4. Have students design a book cover (front and back and inside flaps) for *A Tale of Two Cities*.

5. Have students design a bulletin board (ready to be put up; not just sketched) for *A Tale of Two Cities*.

6. Expand the last option from Writing Assignment #2 to a whole-class group project. Divide your class into X number of groups. Have each group create a video about your town/city, complete with narration. Each person in each group should have specific tasks to do. The entire group should decide what will be in the video and in what order the things should be presented. One person should do the camera work, one or two people should write the script for the narration, one person should be in charge of any research necessary, etc.

7. Have students choose one chapter of the book (with sufficient dialogue) to rewrite as a play. In conjunction with this assignment, have students write a composition explaining the difficulties they encountered in changing from one written form to another.

8. Hold a mock trial of your own in which Charles Darnay is put on trial for the infractions of his family against the working class. Have students work out who will prosecute, who will defend, who will be witnesses, and the entire scenario of the trial.

9. Have students take a look at the problems in your neighborhood, town or city. Have students create a campaign to combat at least one problem. Perhaps you could divide your class into groups, and each group could create a campaign for different problems. For example, Group 1 could make a campaign against drugs, another group could create a campaign against litter, another group could make a campaign for recycling, etc.

WORD SEARCH - *A Tale of Two Cities*

All words in this list are associated with *A Tale of Two Cities*. The words are placed backwards, forward, diagonally, up and down. The included words are listed below the word searches.

```
B C R U N C H E R M A R Q U I S E U Q C A J S C
D A V E N G E A N C E X P V G X N L J L Y N H H
G V S E N G L A N D K J T I G T S O L G E A M H
E N I T O L L I U G E N D R Z X G X S K R C J Y
Q V S F I J Z K M T D Y I R P J R L C L C Q B Q
F K J T R L K J T K E N R T V V N I E R L D X M
F B H W R T L E C S O I F Z T M D S R T M E P J
L M Q K K Y N E C S K S C Z K I C L L K T V T X
C L S N X A V X A A G P D U Z Y N F C Z N E T H
M A D A M E D E F A R G E L L E C G N I Y A R P
C R S R T L R N R O B M L C N Y E M Y Q L E B C
J C D E D T F E S Q T O A O J F L L N E W R F B
R O S E S A C S K S E A D G R F O U L O N T W O
K R F S N N S H E J I N G I N R B X T E S D C G
Q I V W A I K R I P O R W N E O Y Q B Q B I Y G
L C S R W B W M A L M H A F N S L L M S X A R S
W D F B S R M G D B D W L P N P S E P F B Q G P
```

BANK	DICKENS	LONDON	STRYVER
BARSAD	DIGS	LORRY	SYDNEY
BASTILLE	DRMANETTE	LUCIE	TALE
BODIES	ENGLAND	MADAMEDEFARGE	TELLSONS
CARMAGNOLE	FOULON	MARQUIS	TOWER
CASES	FRANCE	PARIS	TREASON
CASK	GABELLE	PRAYING	TWO
CELL	GUILLOTINE	VENGEANCE	PRISON
CHARLES	JACQUES	PROSS	WINE
CHILD	KNITTING	REST	CLY
LETTER	ROSE	CRUNCHER	LIFE
SEA			

KEY: WORD SEARCH - *A Tale of Two Cities*

All words in this list are associated with *A Tale of Two Cities*. The words are placed backwards, forward, diagonally, up and down. The included words are listed below the word searches.

```
        B C R U N C H E R M A R Q U I S E U Q C A J S C
          A V E N G E A N C E       G   N         N H
            S E N G L A N D K     I       O     E A
        E N I T O L L I U G E N D           S K R
            S I       T     I           L C L
              T L     T   E N   T       I E   L
                R   L E       O I     T   D S   T       E
                  K   Y N E C S       C     I       K T   T
        C   S       A V   A A     P   U Y N         N E T
        M A D A M E D E F A R G E L L E C G N I Y A R P
        C     S R       R   R O B M L C N     E   Y   L E B
              D E D T   E S     T O A O         L N E W
        R O S E S A C S     S E A D G R F O U L O N T W O
              F   N N S H E   I N   I N R       T E S D
                I   A I   R I   O R       E O Y     B I Y
            L     R     W   A L       A     S L         A R S
                    F             B D     P       E       G P
```

BANK	DICKENS	LONDON	STRYVER
BARSAD	DIGS	LORRY	SYDNEY
BASTILLE	DRMANETTE	LUCIE	TALE
BODIES	ENGLAND	MADAMEDEFARGE	TELLSONS
CARMAGNOLE	FOULON	MARQUIS	TOWER
CASES	FRANCE	PARIS	TREASON
CASK	GABELLE	PRAYING	TWO
CELL	GUILLOTINE	VENGEANCE	PRISON
CHARLES	JACQUES	PROSS	WINE
CHILD	KNITTING	REST	CLY
LETTER	ROSE	CRUNCHER	LIFE
SEA			

CROSSWORD - A Tale of Two Cities

CROSSWORD CLUES - *A Tale of Two Cities*

ACROSS

1. Madame Defarge wants total extermination of them
6. Solomon Pross
9. Spy; supposed to be dead
10. Darnay; renounces his family's name
13. Tellson's, for example
15. Carton prepared Stryver's
17. "Let them eat grass."
19. Jerry was a messenger there
22. Takes Lucie to her father
23. Cruncher does this in his spare time
26. Madame Defarge's Lieutenant
30. One Hundred and Five, North ____
32. What Cruncher 'fishes' for
34. A signal that a spy is in the shop
35. Marries Charles
36. Lucie's friend/servant
37. Jerry calls this 'flopping

DOWN

2. "...it is a far, far better ____ that I go to"
3. Dickens' metaphor for the mob
4. Dance of the mob
5. ____ of Two Cities
6. A prison
7. The people of France were having one
8. Author
10. A ____ of wine spilled in the street
11. "Recalled to ____"
12. A Tale of ____ Cities
14. Madame Defarge's pasttime
15. Jail cubicle
16. Carton; takes Darnay's place at the guillotine
17. Country in which Paris is located
18. Mr. Manette's was damaging to Darnay
20. English city
21. Jerry; part-time grave robber
24. Carton's employer; attorney
25. Darnay was being tried for this crime
27. Country in which London is located
28. Asked Charles to come to France
29. One of the two cities
31. Kind of shop Defarge kept

ANSWER KEY CROSSWORD *A Tale of Two Cities*

MATCHING QUIZ/WORKSHEET 1 - *A Tale of Two Cities*

_____ 1. LIFE   A. Carton; Takes Darnay's place at the guillotine

_____ 2. PRAYING   B. Kind of shop Defarge kept

_____ 3. CELL   C. Dance of the mob

_____ 4. GABELLE   D. A signal that a spy is in the shop

_____ 5. CASK   E. A ____ of wine spilled in the street

_____ 6. FOULON   F. Darnay; Renounces his family's name

_____ 7. PROSS   G. Jerry calls this 'flopping'

_____ 8. BASTILLE   H. Carton prepared Stryver's

_____ 9. PARIS   I. Asked Charles to come to France

_____ 10. SYDNEY   J. 'Recalled to ____'

_____ 11. MARQUIS   K. Jail cubicle

_____ 12. ROSE   L. Used to cut off heads

_____ 13. CASES   M. Cobbling

_____ 14. CARMAGNOLE   N. St. Evremonde; Darnay's uncle

_____ 15. WINE   O. The carriage of the Marquis ran over one

_____ 16. CHILD   P. A prison

_____ 17. KNITTING   Q. One of the two cities

_____ 18. GUILLOTINE R. Lucie's friend/servant

_____ 19. DR MANETTE S. Madame Defarge's pastime

_____ 20. CHARLES   T. 'Let them eat grass.'

KEY: MATCHING QUIZ/WORKSHEET 1 - *A Tale of Two Cities*

J	1. LIFE	A. Carton; Takes Darnay's place at the guillotine
G	2. PRAYING	B. Kind of shop Defarge kept
K	3. CELL	C. Dance of the mob
I	4. GABELLE	D. A signal that a spy is in the shop
E	5. CASK	E. A ____ of wine spilled in the street
T	6. FOULON	F. Darnay; Renounces his family's name
R	7. PROSS	G. Jerry calls this 'flopping'
P	8. BASTILLE	H. Carton prepared Stryver's
Q	9. PARIS	I. Asked Charles to come to France
A	10. SYDNEY	J. 'Recalled to ____'
N	11. MARQUIS	K. Jail cubicle
D	12. ROSE	L. Used to cut off heads
H	13. CASES	M. Cobbling
C	14. CARMAGNOLE	N. St. Evremonde; Darnay's uncle
B	15. WINE	O. The carriage of the Marquis ran over one
O	16. CHILD	P. A prison
S	17. KNITTING	Q. One of the two cities
L	18. GUILLOTINE	R. Lucie's friend/servant
M	19. DR MANETTE	S. Madame Defarge's pastime
F	20. CHARLES	T. 'Let them eat grass.'

MATCHING QUIZ/WORKSHEET 2 - *A Tale of Two Cities*

_____ 1. ENGLAND   A. One of the two cities

_____ 2. TOWER   B. One Hundred and Five, North _____

_____ 3. PRAYING   C. Takes Lucie to her father

_____ 4. FOULON   D. Jerry calls this 'flopping'

_____ 5. TALE   E. Carton prepared Stryver's

_____ 6. LORRY   F. Country in which London is situated

_____ 7. BASTILLE   G. 'Let them eat grass.'

_____ 8. CRUNCHER   H. Dickens' metaphor for the mob

_____ 9. GABELLE   I. A prison

_____ 10. PARIS   J. Country in which Paris is situated

_____ 11. TREASON   K. _____ of Two Cities

_____ 12. CASES   L. A Tale of _____ Cities

_____ 13. FRANCE   M. Jerry; part-time grave robber

_____ 14. BODIES   N. Madame Defarge's pastime

_____ 15. ERNEST DEFARGE   O. Darnay was being tried for this crime

_____ 16. KNITTING   P. Madame Defarge's lieutenant

_____ 17. TWO   Q. Kind of shop Defarge kept

_____ 18. WINE   R. What Cruncher 'fishes' for

_____ 19. SEA   S. Asked Charles to come to France

_____ 20. VENGEANCE   T. Wine shop keeper

KEY: MATCHING QUIZ/WORKSHEET 2 - *A Tale of Two Cities*

F	1. ENGLAND	A. One of the two cities
B	2. TOWER	B. One Hundred and Five, North _____
D	3. PRAYING	C. Takes Lucie to her father
G	4. FOULON	D. Jerry calls this 'flopping'
K	5. TALE	E. Carton prepared Stryver's
C	6. LORRY	F. Country in which London is situated
I	7. BASTILLE	G. 'Let them eat grass.'
M	8. CRUNCHER	H. Dickens' metaphor for the mob
S	9. GABELLE	I. A prison
A	10. PARIS	J. Country in which Paris is situated
O	11. TREASON	K. _____ of Two Cities
E	12. CASES	L. A Tale of _____ Cities
J	13. FRANCE	M. Jerry; part-time grave robber
R	14. BODIES	N. Madame Defarge's pastime
T	15. ERNEST DEFARGE	O. Darnay was being tried for this crime
N	16. KNITTING	P. Madame Defarge's lieutenant
L	17. TWO	Q. Kind of shop Defarge kept
Q	18. WINE	R. What Cruncher 'fishes' for
H	19. SEA	S. Asked Charles to come to France
P	20. VENGEANCE	T. Wine shop keeper

REVIEW GAME CLUE SHEET - *A Tale of Two Cities*

SCRAMBLED	WORD	CLUE
ANCFER	FRANCE	Country in which Paris is situated
IKENDSC	DICKENS	Author
ATEL	TALE	___ of Two Cities
LYC	CLY	Spy; supposed to be dead
ESBILALT	BASTILLE	A prison
RWEOT	TOWER	One Hundred and Five, North_____
EAS	SEA	Dickens' metaphor for the mob
ILUEC	LUCIE	Marries Charles
SPSRO	PROSS	Lucie's friend/servant
ARSDAB	BARSAD	Solomon Pross
DAENFGESRETRE	ERNESTDEFARGE	Wine shop keeper
AKCS	CASK	A_____ of wine spilled in the street
GTNTINIK	KNITTING	Madam Defarge's pastime
RLOYR	LORRY	Takes Lucie to her father
EBGELAL	GABELLE	Asked Charles to come to France
ICHDL	CHILD	The Marquis' carriage ran over one
NEWI	WINE	Kind of shop Defarge kept
NIROPS	PRISON	Lucie's father had been there 18 years
ECASS	CASES	Carton prepared Stryver's
IORCSSRTAAT	ARISTOCRATS	Madam Defarge wants their total extermination

VOCABULARY RESOURCE MATERIALS

VOCABULARY WORD SEARCH - *A Tale of Two Cities*

All words in this list are associated with *A Tale of Two Cities* with an emphasis on the vocabulary words chosen for study in the text. The words are placed backwards, forward, diagonally, up and down. The included words are listed below.

```
A N T I P A T H Y A P A N H H B G H X S L D H M
R I S M H C L K Y M S Y L G Y F T T Q M C B T X
Y H N G R S B A J S G S L A X C H S N Z L D B C
S T E E P E D A C Q U I E S C E N C E E T A B A
H D I S X O T I E I X N N U R T A L F V T H Q
S Z E C I O R I S L T S F E T O I B D B I R M F
Z U L B A M R T N C B S N A N E I T X N S N E R
I B P H A G O A E U E A I O T G D B Y N U Q A F
Y M J P B U A T B N E R B E I H E T U P M D Q M
O R P S L S C S A L T L N R H T O N B D W Z E N
R B X E Q I F H A N E O R I U T A M D P P H B R
W B L M R K C R E N A O U G B T A C A E D N N G
R B C I J I T A I R C K G S W L R R O B R D J L
C N X B V C O E T N Y G Q M L X E E D V L E W R
F Q N W E I N U I I M P L J X Y G Q P B A E D P
X F Y P H T O L S U O I C I R P A C X M V F L F
D I S S O N A N C E V N W P Y Y W T L K I L L N
```

ABATE	CAPRICIOUS	IMPERTURBABLE	RETINUE
ACQUIESCENCE	DEBAUCHERY	INCORRIGIBLE	SAGACITY
ALACRITY	DISCERNIBLE	INEXORABLE	SPECTRAL
ANATOMISE	DISSONANCE	LENIENT	STEEPED
ANTIPATHY	DUBIOUSLY	MANIFEST	SUPPLICATION
ASSENTED	ENGENDERED	OBLIVION	UNFATHOMABLE
ATHEISTICAL	FERVENT	PORTENTOUSLY	
AVOCATIONS	IMPERIOUS	REDUNDANCY	

KEY: VOCABULARY WORD SEARCH - *A Tale of Two Cities*

All words in this list are associated with *A Tale of Two Cities* with an emphasis on the vocabulary words chosen for study in the text. The words are placed backwards, forward, diagonally, up and down. The included words are listed below.

```
        A  N  T  I  P  A  T  H  Y  A        A
           I        L           S  Y  L  Y     T  T
        Y     N     R     A     S  L  A  C     S  N
        S  T  E  E  P  E  D  A  C  Q  U  I  E  S  C  E  N  C  E  E  T  A  B  A
           D  I  S  X  O  T  I  E  I     N     N  U  R     A  L  F  V
        S     E  C  I  O  R  I  S  L  T  S  F  E  T  O  I  B  D     I  R
           U     B  A  M  R  T  N  C  B  S  N  A  N  E  I  T     N     N  E
        I     P     A  G  O  A  E  U  E  A  I  O  T  G  D  B  Y     U     A  F
           M     P     U  A  T  B  N  E  R  B  E  I  H  E     U        D     M
        O     P     L     C  S  A  L  T  L  N  R  H  T  O  N     D           E
           B     E     I     H  A  N  E  O  R  I  U  T  A  M  D                 R
              L     R     C  R  E  N  A  O  U     B  T  A  C  A  E
                 I     I  T  A  I  R  C        S     L  R     O  B  R
                    V  C  O  E  T  N  Y           L     E  E     V  L  E
                    E  I  N  U  I  I                 Y        P     A  E  D
                    P     T  O     S  U  O  I  C  I  R  P  A  C     M
        D  I  S  S  O  N  A  N  C  E        N                              I
```

ABATE	CAPRICIOUS	IMPERTURBABLE	RETINUE
ACQUIESCENCE	DEBAUCHERY	INCORRIGIBLE	SAGACITY
ALACRITY	DISCERNIBLE	INEXORABLE	SPECTRAL
ANATOMISE	DISSONANCE	LENIENT	STEEPED
ANTIPATHY	DUBIOUSLY	MANIFEST	SUPPLICATION
ASSENTED	ENGENDERED	OBLIVION	UNFATHOMABLE
ATHEISTICAL	FERVENT	PORTENTOUSLY	
AVOCATIONS	IMPERIOUS	REDUNDANCY	

VOCABULARY CROSSWORD - *A Tale of Two Cities*

VOCABULARY CROSSWORD CLUES - *A Tale of Two Cities*

ACROSS
1. State of being forgotten
4. Evident; obvious
7. 'Recalled to _____'
8. Dislike; opposition
10. Whimsical
14. Unbending; unrelenting
17. Occupations
20. Compliance
22. _____ of Two Cities
23. To lessen
24. Making motions (usually with hands) while speaking
25. A train of attendants
27. Jail cubicle
28. Soaked
30. Dickens' metaphor for the mob
31. Carton prepared Stryver's
34. Carton's employer; attorney
36. 'Let them eat grass.'
37. Tellson's, for example
38. Madame Defarge wants total extermination of them

DOWN
2. Having an indulgent, mild disposition
3. Spy; supposed to be dead
5. Earnest
6. Discord; disagreement in sound
9. Dissect; analyze
11. Not believing in God
12. Bad beyond correction or reform
13. Distinguishable
15. A Tale of ____ Cities
16. Ambitious display; great showing of something
18. Agreed
19. Habitual bad conduct
20. Liveliness; cheerful readiness
21. To be caused or produced
26. Darnay was being tried for this crime
29. Cruncher does this in his spare time
31. A ____ of wine spilled in the street
32. Solomon Pross
33. A signal that a spy is in the shop
35. '...it is a far, far better ___ that I go to....'

VOCABULARY CROSSWORD ANSWER KEY

VOCABULARY WORKSHEET 1 - *A Tale of Two Cities*

____ 1. Not believing in God
    A. discernible   B. vociferating   C. oblivion   D. atheistical

____ 2. Using or having more than necessary
    A. redundancy   B. engendered   C. imperious   D. antipathy

____ 3. Humble begging
    A. supplication   B. anatomise   C. manifest   D. fervent

____ 4. Having an indulgent, mild disposition
    A. lenient   B. fervent   C. acquiescence   D. spectral

____ 5. State of being forgotten
    A. approbation   B. capricious   C. anatomise   D. oblivion

____ 6. Compliance
    A. discernible   B. engendered   C. acquiescence   D. avocations

____ 7. Ghostly
    A. avocations   B. spectral   C. acquiescence   D. inexorable

____ 8. To lessen
    A. anatomise   B. capricious   C. abate   D. sagacity

____ 9. Dissect; analyze
    A. abate   B. imperious   C. anatomise   D. assented

____ 10. Unmovable; calm; can't be bothered
    A. imperturbable   B. assented   C. approbation   D. imperious

____ 11. Soaked
    A. incorrigible   B. steeped   C. approbation   D. supplication

____ 12. A train of attendants
    A. retinue   B. dissonance   C. antipathy   D. avocations

____ 13. Bad beyond correction or reform
    A. engendered   B. dissonance   C. incorrigible   D. gesticulation

____ 14. Agreed
    A. atheistical   B. discernible   C. assented   D. propitiate

____ 15. Atone; make amends
    A. manifest   B. propitiate   C. capricious   D. ostentatious

____ 16. Uncertain; doubtful
    A. inexorable   B. dubiously   C. unfathomable   D. spectral

____ 17. To be caused or produced
    A. sagacity   B. imperious   C. engendered   D. imperturbable

____ 18. Incomprehensible; beyond belief
    A. unfathomable   B. oblivion   C. supplication   D. lenient

____ 19. Haughty; arrogant; domineering
    A. retinue   B. imperious   C. discernible   D. imperturbable

____ 20. Making motions (usually with hands) while speaking
    A. gesticulation   B. retinue   C. dubiously   D. abate

ANSWER KEY VOCABULARY WORKSHEET 1 - *A Tale of Two Cities*

__D__ 1. Not believing in God
    A. discernible   B. vociferating   C. oblivion   D. atheistical

__A__ 2. Using or having more than necessary
    A. redundancy   B. engendered   C. imperious   D. antipathy

__A__ 3. Humble begging
    A. supplication   B. anatomise   C. manifest   D. fervent

__A__ 4. Having an indulgent, mild disposition
    A. lenient   B. fervent   C. acquiescence   D. spectral

__D__ 5. State of being forgotten
    A. approbation   B. capricious   C. anatomise   D. oblivion

__C__ 6. Compliance
    A. discernible   B. engendered   C. acquiescence   D. avocations

__B__ 7. Ghostly
    A. avocations   B. spectral   C. acquiescence   D. inexorable

__C__ 8. To lessen
    A. anatomise   B. capricious   C. abate   D. sagacity

__C__ 9. Dissect; analyze
    A. abate   B. imperious   C. anatomise   D. assented

__A__ 10. Unmovable; calm; can't be bothered
    A. imperturbable   B. assented   C. approbation   D. imperious

__B__ 11. Soaked
    A. incorrigible   B. steeped   C. approbation   D. supplication

__A__ 12. A train of attendants
    A. retinue   B. dissonance   C. antipathy   D. avocations

__C__ 13. Bad beyond correction or reform
    A. engendered   B. dissonance   C. incorrigible   D. gesticulation

__C__ 14. Agreed
    A. atheistical   B. discernible   C. assented   D. propitiate

__B__ 15. Atone; make amends
    A. manifest   B. propitiate   C. capricious   D. ostentatious

__B__ 16. Uncertain; doubtful
    A. inexorable   B. dubiously   C. unfathomable   D. spectral

__C__ 17. To be caused or produced
    A. sagacity   B. imperious   C. engendered   D. imperturbable

__A__ 18. Incomprehensible; beyond belief
    A. unfathomable   B. oblivion   C. supplication   D. lenient

__B__ 19. Haughty; arrogant; domineering
    A. retinue   B. imperious   C. discernible   D. imperturbable

__A__ 20. Making motions (usually with hands) while speaking
    A. gesticulation   B. retinue   C. dubiously   D. abate

VOCABULARY WORKSHEET 2 - *A Tale of Two Cities*

___ 1. Sagacity   a. Evident; obvious

___ 2. Approbation   b. Haughty; arrogant; domineering

___ 3. Steeped   c. Approval; liking

___ 4. Retinue   d. To lessen

___ 5. Avocations   e. Dislike; opposition

___ 6. Oblivion   f. Habitual bad conduct

___ 7. Incorrigible   g. Humble begging

___ 8. Supplication   h. State of being forgotten

___ 9. Fervent   i. Earnest

___ 10. Abate   j. Ominously; foreshadowing something bad

___ 11. Anatomise   k. Agreed

___ 12. Spectral   l. Ghostly

___ 13. Manifest   m. Not believing in God

___ 14. Antipathy   n. Compliance

___ 15. Assented   o. Shrewdness; intelligence

___ 16. Debauchery   p. Occupations

___ 17. Atheistical   q. Bad beyond correction or reform

___ 18. Imperious   r. A train of attendants

___ 19. Portentously   s. Dissect; analyze

___ 20. Acquiescence   t. Soaked

KEY: VOCABULARY WORKSHEET 2 - *A Tale of Two Cities*

O 1. Sagacity   a. Evident; obvious

C 2. Approbation   b. Haughty; arrogant; domineering

T 3. Steeped   c. Approval; liking

R 4. Retinue   d. To lessen

P 5. Avocations   e. Dislike; opposition

H 6. Oblivion   f. Habitual bad conduct

Q 7. Incorrigible   g. Humble begging

G 8. Supplication   h. State of being forgotten

I 9. Fervent   i. Earnest

D 10. Abate   j. Ominously; foreshadowing something bad

S 11. Anatomise   k. Agreed

L 12. Spectral   l. Ghostly

A 13. Manifest   m. Not believing in God

E 14. Antipathy   n. Compliance

K 15. Assented   o. Shrewdness; intelligence

F 16. Debauchery   p. Occupations

M 17. Atheistical   q. Bad beyond correction or reform

B 18. Imperious   r. A train of attendants

J 19. Portentously   s. Dissect; analyze

N 20. Acquiescence   t. Soaked

VOCABULARY JUGGLE LETTER REVIEW GAME CLUES - *A Tale of Two Cities*

SCRAMBLED	WORD	CLUE
ILENNTE	LENIENT	indulgent, mild disposition
LCTIAYRA	ALACRITY	liveliness; cheerful readiness
SEASNOCIND	DISSONANCE	discord; disagreement in sound
LOUIATNSPPCI	SUPPLICATION	humble begging
SUEROMPII	IMPERIOUS	haughty; arrogant; domineering
CLTSAEPR	SPECTRAL	ghostly
EGRBICONRLII	INCORRIGIBLE	bad beyond correction or reform
SMFNTAEI	MANIFEST	evident; obvious
TUERENI	RETINUE	a train of attendants
EDEETSP	STEEPED	soaked
TIETOPAPIR	PROPITIATE	atone; make amends
SIEHTAACTLI	ATHEISTICAL	not believing in God
APEMERLBRBUIT	IMPERTURBABLE	unmovable; calm; can't be bothered
OAISTENMA	ANATOMISE	dissect; analyze
YCEEBAURHD	DEBAUCHERY	habitual bad conduct
NETEVRF	FERVENT	earnest
UTTSAESTNIOO	OSTENTATIOUS	ambitious display; great showing of something
NEDSTESA	ASSENTED	agreed
IOOBINLV	OBLIVION	state of being forgotten
SCAAINTOVO	AVOCATIONS	occupations